AGING
AGELESSLY

AGING
AGELESSLY

Busting the Myth of Age-Related Mental Decline

Tony Buzan & Raymond Keen

Foreword by Jean Buzan

MEDIA

MEDIA

Published 2023 by Gildan Media LLC
aka G&D Media
www.GandDmedia.com

AGING AGELESSLY © 2023 Tony Buzan International Limited
Rights licensed exclusively by JMW Group, Inc. All rights reserved.

Front cover design by David Rheinhardt of Pyrographx

Designed by Meghan Day Healey of Story Horse, LLC.

Library of Congress Cataloging-in-Publication Data is available upon request

ISBN: 978-1-7225-0638-4

10 9 8 7 6 5 4 3 2 1

Contents

Foreword

by Jean Buzan, MA

You're not getting older. You're getting better.
Many of us still believe the widespread delusions about our mental capacity declining as we age. Do you still think that your brain cells die off daily throughout your life? That your brain power diminishes as you age, until finally, if you live long enough, you decline into "senility"?

I did for many years, and if you do, then join a club of billions.

It isn't that the experts deliberately misled us—they really believed what they were saying. The story goes that, at a postmortem years ago, two young doctors remarked that, in general, older people's brains weighed a little less than those of younger people. "That accounts for their failing mental capacities," remarked one. From this reasonable, but unscientific, deduction, the assumption became an accepted "fact."

The story may be apocryphal, but the theory that we lose millions of brain cells on a continuing basis has been widely accepted for years. To too great an extent, it still is.

Change Your Life

The recently discovered truth is far more palatable, and knowing it can change a person's whole life.

First, our minds/intellect/intelligence do not consist of a limited number of brain cells, which die daily and cannot be renewed. The abilities of that incredible 3½-pound (1.6-kilogram) computer in your head are produced by the number of interconnections made between those cells. And that number, dear brain owner, is infinite in its growth potential!

So, you ask, what about the reduction in weight at post-mortems? I would propose that this is due merely to the overall reduction in body fluid as one ages physically. I would also propose that it is not inevitable. After all, how many of us really drink eight glasses of water daily, as we are encouraged to do?

There was another, more serious reason why this delusion was so widely accepted. When IQ testing first began, psychologists carried out studies comparing older and younger groups, and "proved" that the latter were far more intelligent. Therefore, they concluded, mental functioning declines with age.

These cross-sectional studies were carried out in a very simple fashion—in fact too simple! Two groups—one of older people and one of younger—were each given a time-limited IQ test. Since the younger groups consistently performed better than the older groups, the conclusion was that a person's intellectual capacity must, therefore, deteriorate with age.

Then some bright psychologist tried removing the time limit. The older people took a little longer, but performed significantly better—comparably with those of the younger groups. The extra time needed was accounted for by two facts—the older people were unfamiliar with the type of tests used, which were commonplace to younger people; and the older peoples' brains contained more years of experience and therefore had more information to process when considering the questions.

> ## Brain Flash: Design Your Own Aging Process
> Aging is not identical with fate; individuals play a major role in designing their own process of aging.
> —*Successful Aging: Perspectives from the Behavioral Sciences*, by Paul B. and Margaret M. Baltes

Eventually, psychologists devised a longitudinal intelligence test, whereby they tested a person annually for many years, comparing the results of the same people against themselves. And guess what? In many ways their results improved over the years.

Think what this exciting new information means. Providing that you believe in yourself and continue to stimulate your brain, it really is true that you're not getting older, you're getting better!

The Power of Free Will
Professor David Suzuki, a geneticist at the University of British Columbia (now retired), has persuasively argued that although genes do play a fundamental role in determining human character, "The really important genes are not the

ones which tell us what to do, but the ones that give us the ability to change behavior in response to our environment."

In other words, there are genes that create what we recognize as free will. Suzuki claims that the whole evolution of higher mammals is the story of genes handing over control to the brain, so that people have become more and more capable of behaving independently of their genes.

The contradiction between free will and determinism has run throughout philosophical debate from early times to our own, taking on different forms at different stages. The seventeenth-century philosopher Baruch Spinoza, for example, in his work *Ethics*, argued that there is no such thing as free will and that circumstances are ruled by absolute logical necessity: everything that happens is a manifestation of God's nature, and it is logically impossible that events should be other than they are. Other philosophers were less happy with this rigidly deterministic framework, which seems to place us in a clockwork universe, where "God" releases the spring at the start of time and we all shuffle along predetermined paths until that spring finally winds down.

A different aspect of this argument is the nature versus nurture debate. Are we all little more than a distillation of the genetic material of our forebears, or are we capable of being molded by the influences to which we are exposed in our own environment? Those of a deterministic inclination would probably argue that the most accurate indicator of human potential is the genetic hand dealt to them at conception, and that there is little that can be done to alter this. Clearly this is going to be an important factor, particularly in terms of physical development: if the parents are both below average height, their offspring is unlikely to become a basketball champion. In terms of mental development, however, the brain is capable of assimilating phenomenal amounts of information, and the more it is stimulated, the more it will have the potential to achieve at any age! In chapter 4, for example, we introduce the important TEFCAS model, with its emphasis on your ability to change and adjust.

In this book the authors explore the growing body of information that supports the theory that the brain thrives on stimulation. The more it gets, the more powerfully it evolves—at every stage of its development.

Potential Leonardos

Every human being is a potential Leonardo da Vinci!

Even the great Renaissance sculptor Michelangelo described his work as merely "freeing the image that already existed inside the block of stone." It is possible to view ongoing human development in the same terms.

If you use your brain as it should be used—and the authors map out an appropriate strategy in this book—the potential for developing your brain is limitless.

Brain Flash
Vital Factors in Aging Gracefully

History offers ample instances of brilliance in life's later years, from Michelangelo to Martha Graham. The key factors include:

- **Staying socially involved.** Among those who decline, deterioration is most rapid in older people who withdraw from life.

- **Being mentally active.** Well-educated people who continue their intellectual interests tend to increase their verbal intelligence through old age.
- **Having a flexible personality.** A study found that people most able to tolerate ambiguity and enjoy new experiences in middle age maintained their mental alertness best through old age.

The new view is accompanied by data attacking the notion that the brain degenerates precipitously with aging. The widespread belief that there is devastating cell loss in the elderly brain—and the related claim that each drink of liquor destroys a large number of brain cells—seems now to be unfounded. Marion Diamond, a neuroanatomist at the University of Berkeley, tried to track down the source of the belief and could find no definitive study proving it.

—International Herald Tribune

Swimming Records Prove That Age Is No Barrier to Speed

December 2021 statistics from the World Masters Swimming Division (long course) show that the men's record in the 50 meters Freestyle 35–39 years old section is 22.76 seconds; 55–59 years, 24.45 seconds, and 80–84 years, 31.96 seconds. The physical decline with age is amazingly small. Women records are on average 3–5 seconds slower at all stages but maintain a similarly small rate of decline.

Introduction

No one under the age of forty is permitted to read my book.
—MOSES MAIMONIDES (1135–1204) ON HIS BOOK
A GUIDE FOR THE PERPLEXED

*Everyone from 8 to 118 and beyond is
positively encouraged to read our book.*
—TONY BUZAN AND RAY KEENE

Aging Agelessly is aimed primarily at the generations now in their forties and fifties, the so-called Gen Xers and Gen Yers, who form such a massive global presence in the world's developed nations. However, we are also addressing the over-fifties, who still have serious ambitions to succeed. Of course, any book that gives advice on improving mental powers can be equally applicable to an eight-year-old or an eighty-year-old, or even a 118-year-old! It is never too early, or too late, to start.

The core of the book is practical advice aimed directly at you, the reader, targeting your aspirations for the future, as well as your fears, and proposing solutions. You undoubtedly want to know what you can do to extend your physical and mental fitness beyond middle age, to resist the onslaught of younger generations, and to reverse the negative stereotypes you routinely encounter, such as "Experience is no substitute for youthful energy and adaptability." In short, you want to maximize your personal potential and *not be thrown on the scrapheap* simply because the years are gathering pace.

We illustrate our advice with shining examples of superlative achievements in advanced age—anecdotes of this nature spice and pepper the text to inspire you.

Our book does three things:

1. It strikes a resounding note with the aging population worldwide. It addresses your concerns about aging with a clarion call that you cannot ignore and will instantly recognize as your own.

2. It offers a host of ideas for stimulating your brain, motivating you to stay fit and healthy. Remember: the more you stimulate your mind, the more you will be capable of achieving.

3. It reinforces the message with real-life precedents showing what can be achieved by those who start on the path to success later in life: for instance, by those who have only truly learned how to learn, or how to think for themselves, well past the end of their formal school or college education. And we record the exploits of those who have made, or continue to make, their mark in great age. Such inspirational examples include the 100-year-old Australian grandmother who broke a swimming record, and the self-defense of the ninety-year-old Greek dramatist Sophocles against his son's predatory lawsuit.

**Brain Flash
The Costly Lament of Britain's
Discarded 50-Somethings**

This year, many of my friends are reaching 50. One or two, riding high in affluence and achievement, are holding good parties. But their guests reveal a different story. For many more, the half-century is bringing an end to careers they thought would go on a lot longer and, they hoped, further. To their amazement, they are cast as the fat being shed in the latest corporate diet plan. Some are victims of multinationals' mass culls of middle-rank executives, when age is often the first parameter fed into the search program. Professionals, sidelined from the fee-earning mainstream to make way for young bloods, find they are an embarrassment when overheads have to be cut. A generation of nearly-men—and it is usually men—are falling off the corporate pyramid.

—Graham Sargeant in *The* [London] *Times*

Challenging Conventional Wisdom

Now, more than ever before in previous societies, there is a cult of youth and a tendency to throw fifty- (or even forty-) somethings on the scrapheap to make way for the young.

Yet everything we have learned contradicts this piece of conventional wisdom. Time and again, during our decades-long research into the great minds of the past and present, we have been struck by the extraordinary force, vigor, ambition, and sheer drive exhibited by people at an age when human beings are conventionally meant to slow down. We also note, amazingly, that the work of the great geniuses tended to improve as they got older. This was the case with Goethe, Shakespeare, Beethoven, and Michelangelo. In many instances, their supreme masterpiece was their final work, produced in extreme old age.

Coauthor Tony Buzan was also becoming increasingly impressed, on his worldwide lecture tours, by his older listeners' inquisitiveness and readiness to learn. Again, this perception contradicted the current stereotype of the older person's resistance to new information and techniques.

The Scientific and Medical Evidence on Aging

The evidence we found, which is cited in this book, is most encouraging for our new view of aging. Multiple sources of evidence indicate that by using the brain well and properly as you get older, you physically change it, improving and streamlining its synaptic connections and hence its powers of association.

The autopsy on Einstein's brain after his death is a case in point. Einstein's brain revealed that it contained 400 percent more glial cells than the norm. Since these cells specifically aid interconnectivity in the brain circuits, the effect would have been to boost his power of association between apparently separate items far beyond the average. Of course, Einstein may have been exceptional in this respect, but it is encouraging for all of us.

The Benefits of Constant Challenge

We shall dispel the misconceptions that exist about the inevitable decline of the brain as age increases. It is popularly believed that one loses millions of brain cells every day through the attrition of encroaching age. This is simply not true. It is an old myth that has been passed around in circular fashion, with no substantive evidence whatsoever for it. We refute this harmful lie, citing proof from well-researched scientific sources. In fact, synaptic connections can be physically improved by proper exercise of the brain. Constant challenge and problem-solving will physically improve your brain.

Wiser with Age

Previous human societies developed various reverential names for the old, for example: *patriarchs, matriarchs, oracles, the wise, elders, sages,* and *seers.* In contrast, in modern society, the personality characteristics commonly attributed to the aged are stereotypical negatives, such as *obstinate, pigheaded,* and *inflexible.*

How did this state of affairs come about? Such negative expressions are simply reversals of what should be seen as positive qualities. *Stubborn* should, for instance, be reinterpreted as *determined.* It is important to redefine the derogatory terms to reveal the positives that underlie them.

Ways to Improve Your Brain

Naturally we recommend physical exercise with an aerobic element, as well as stressing the importance of a balanced diet and the harmful effects of smoking and excessive drinking. And, very importantly, we recommend mental exercise too. We advocate mind sports, teasers, and puzzles as brain calisthenics to stretch and challenge your mental powers. Memory and creativity techniques are studied to demonstrate how they can permit fifty-somethings and older to compete with, and outwit, their younger rivals. On another level, current medical thinking indicates that Alzheimer's disease may essentially be a rotting of inactive brains as they get older. We explore this theory and analyze whether there are possible defense systems, or even reversal methods—and what these might be.

Our program consists of practical steps with concrete examples. We aim to encourage our readers to take renewed pride in themselves and challenge and stretch their imaginations, their creativity and, ultimately, their achievements. Readers will inevitably ask: how do I kick myself into action? Here we offer practical advice to help you prevent your brain from deteriorating over time!

Aerobic Exercise at Home

Aerobic exercise is invaluable for increasing the efficiency with which oxygen is transported around the body. There are many forms of aerobic exercise, such as a brisk walk, a strenuous game of squash, swimming, cycling, skipping, and circuit training with weights.

In chapters 7 and 8 we provide extensive guidelines for maintaining and improving your cardiovascular health.

Mind Sports

Having dealt with physical stimulation and stressed the little-recognized fact that the brain is actually part of the body, we move on to the vital area of mental stimulation. One important branch of this comprises mind sports, brainteasers, and puzzles.

It's no mistake that for decades newspapers and magazines have devoted an entire page of their publications to feed the insatiable demand for these brain challenges. Even in today's trimmed-down newspapers and magazines, you often find crossword puzzles, sudoku, word scrambles, chess challenges, and more. Newspaper and magazine editors realize that readers need and crave these items both for amusement and to sharpen their minds.

Memory

We also demonstrate memory systems that can be adapted to simple and effective everyday use. These include the "memory theater" and Tony Buzan's patent specialty, the colorful Mind Map, which helps you to remember complex formulas, lists, lecture material, or notes for tests, exams, or presentations. The Mind Map is fun and exciting, as well as extremely useful.

Creativity

How can you increase your creativity? Most over-forties are widely expected to be suffering from a lessening of their creative drive. It is a commonplace of academia that no worthwhile research in mathematics, for example, is done after the age of twenty-six. In fact, most people are locked into a negative spiral regarding creativity, falsely believing that the higher the number of ideas generated, the more the quality deteriorates—that is, as quantity increases, quality decreases. In this book, we dramatically expose the widespread fallacies about declining creativity. Attendees at Tony Buzan's lectures have described his revelations on this topic as "life-transforming."

Brain Flash
Symbols of Intelligence

Why are mind games, chess in particular, so important to us? Throughout the history of culture, prowess at mind games has been associated with intelligence in general; and mind games have an extraordinary pedigree. According to Dr. Irving Finkel of the Western Asiatic Antiquities department at the British Museum, game boards have been discovered in Palestine and Jordan dating back to Neolithic times, around 7000 BC. Astoundingly, this pre-dates our current knowledge of when writing and pottery were introduced in those societies. Since many of the board games were found in tombs, it is likely that the shades of the departed were believed to play a game with the gods of the underworld to ensure safe conduct into the afterlife.

Board games are no longer regarded as a sort of IQ test for the dead, but they do retain their relevance as symbols of mental prowess.

Smashing the Age Barrier

Current genetic thinking indicates that there is an age cap for human longevity, extending from the age of 85 to perhaps 125 at its outer limit. Citing the latest research, we explore whether this ultimate age barrier can be smashed. This is both a philosophical and a medical question of immense importance.

Sex

We look at the aging brain in relation to sex, love, and romance. Is it better at seventy? We show that, if you stay fit and mentally alert, your sex life, far from declining with the years, will be a source of ever-increasing pleasure.

The Methuselah Mandate: The Golden Oldies

We look at the Great Oldies: notable examples of artists, leaders, mind sports champions and general achievers, whose work clearly improved with age, such as Shakespeare, Goethe, Beethoven, Brahms, and Michelangelo. We spice our text with examples—quirky or fascinating—of extraordinary achievers, such as the nineteenth-century cricketer Charles Absolon, who between the ages of sixty and ninety took 8,500 wickets and scored 26,000 runs in first-class cricket. He captured 500 wickets in just one season at the age of fifty-seven. We also look at amazing performances in mental sports and at the extraordinary records set in the Veterans' Olympics for Physical Sports.

Statistical Records

Statistics show the massive progress and the acceleration in speed, endurance, strength, and flexibility of older generations as they have put effort into their physical health on all levels.

Conclusion

Our central thrust is sensational and reverses conventional thinking! *Your brain improves with age*—if it is used well. We show how it has been done by others and how you can do it for yourself.

If you think about it, our revolutionary new thesis conforms to simple logic: older people have experienced more—not less—than younger people and are therefore more adaptable when retrained or forced to compete in brain power with younger generations.

Maintain Your Competitive Edge

Many people fear retirement, while simultaneously sensing that they have much to offer society in terms of their experience, which is being wasted. *Aging Agelessly* explains clearly, succinctly, and with the latest scientific evidence that *your thinking, creativity, and general potential can increase with age rather than withering.* Many of those with more free time on their hands still passionately believe that they have it in them to achieve dazzling levels of performance. And since "jobs for life" no longer exist, the current trend proves the necessity to adapt and compete. We show you how!

Global Megatrends and You

The world's population is aging. Fertility rates are declining as life expectancy is on the rise. According to the World Health Organization (WHO), "this demographic change has resulted in increasing numbers and proportions of people who are over sixty. As a result, the first time in history when there will be more older people than younger people is rapidly approaching." Many of these "older people" are wondering what the future holds as they enter their forties and fifties. Governments worldwide are also wondering how best to utilize, care for, and benefit from their aging populations. Will older generations become a drain on national and global economies—or a resource? Of the 8 billion people on this planet, soon over 50 percent will be beyond the age of sixty.

We belong to this aging generation. We understand the problems and have devised our own specific solutions. We therefore speak with credibility about our own proposed solutions. We are not producing hypothetical agendas; we are preaching what we practice!

What Should I Do Now?

Read this book! From now on, at the end of each chapter, we give concrete advice and practical steps for your ongoing development. When bodily (and brain) functions decline, they can often be attributed to the following causes, in varying degrees:

1. Inadequate exercise and an unhealthy diet
2. Smoking and excessive drinking
3. Conforming to expected patterns of behavior, such as behaving as you think older people are meant to behave, rather than acting as you actually feel

If you address all the above, you will be able to lead a more fulfilling life. This book is going to tell you what you should, and should not, do to achieve this goal.

If you motivate yourself, strive for constant stimulation, and keep fit and healthy, you can be a superstar too.

Brain Flash
Delaying Retirement

The proportion of the working age population aged between 50 and the state pension age (SPA) [in the U.K.] will increase from 26% in 2012 to 34% in 2050—an increase of over 5.5 million people. This is the result of increases to the SPA, as well as the so called 'baby boomers' reaching this age band.

The productivity and economic success of the UK will therefore be increasingly tied to the productivity and success of its ageing workforce. Encouraging older people to remain in work will help society to support growing numbers of dependents, while providing individuals with the financial and mental resources needed for longer periods of retirement. The employment rate currently declines from 86% for 50-year-olds, to 65% for 60-year-olds and 31% for 65-year-olds. Priority areas include:

- Supporting the aging population to lead fuller and longer working lives. This means examining the factors that are causing employment rates at older ages to vary across the population.
- Adaptations to the workplace. These include addressing negative attitudes to older workers and health needs, improving workplace design, encouraging access to new technologies, and adaptation of human resources policies and working practices.
- Ensuring individuals re-skill throughout their lifetime. As working lives lengthen, and the workplace undergoes major changes, job-related training will become almost as important to people in mid-life as at the beginning of their career. This will require the UK to move toward a model where training and re-skilling opportunities are available throughout people's careers.

—Future of an Ageing Population,
Government Office for Science, U.K.

CHAPTER 1

Genesis of an Idea

*Education is an ornament in prosperity and
a refuge in adversity. It is the best provision for old age.
Educated men and women are as much superior to
the uneducated as the living are to the dead.*

—ARISTOTLE

This chapter explains how the two coauthors at the same time, but in different parts of the globe, became fascinated by the question of why we are constantly being told that the brain packs up at the age of twenty-six, whereas the people we were studying, the great geniuses, were obviously getting better and better with time.

The statistical findings that we came across indicated that the inherent potential of the brain, both atomically and anatomically, is infinitely greater than has generally been assumed. This leads to the inevitable conclusion that the potential for growth throughout a human lifetime has been systematically underestimated by a colossal margin. The hope contained in this information is one of the greatest omens for humankind as we face the challenges of and opportunities inherent in the world's aging population.

The genesis of this book can be traced to three particular moments in time, over a period of more than a decade, which "met" and ignited to create the flame of a new idea.

The First Spore

The first moment was when Tony Buzan was international editor of the magazine of Mensa, the society for those with high IQs. He had been asked to process the information he had been gathering on the human brain and its intelligence and make suggestions based on that information. Here are his findings:

In many diverse disciplines—biochemistry, mathematics, physics, psychology, and philosophy—researchers have found themselves drawn inevitably toward the same vortex: the brain-mind-body problem and the question of the brain's potential. Meanwhile, fringe sciences have been hurling some hefty spanners into the traditional works.

It is now known, beyond doubt, that the mind is a fabric consisting of layers of interlinked networks, which can consciously control heartbeat, oxygen intake, internal organs, and brain waves. There is also evidence that the mind has an even more extensive control over functions than was previously assumed. In deep states of meditation or hypnosis, people have been observed to eliminate pain; paralyze a part of their body completely; produce massive skin eruptions where no cause was apparent (and eliminate them immediately afterwards); induce any predetermined symptom artificially; perform feats of strength normally attributed only to supermen or madmen; and cure themselves of apparently incurable diseases.

In academic circles, researchers have performed experiments in retention and recall, which suggest that the basic storage capacity of the brain is absolute in terms of remembering its own existence. Subjects whose brains were electronically probed produced complete, multisensory recall of situations randomly triggered and ranging over complete lifetimes. In addition, recent work on mnemonic systems indicates that, even without electric interference, the brain can remember a staggering 7,000 disconnected items. It can do this in sequence, in random order, and in reverse order, with no decline in performance as the number of items to be recalled is increased.

In view of this, a complete reassessment of human learning and potential must be made. One of the first considerations is how best to educate an organ—the brain—that is estimated to possess virtually infinite possibilities for associative interconnecting. With such power available to us, it is apparent that our standard, inflexible, linear approaches are no longer acceptable.

It is equally apparent that standard psychological methods of testing ability must be totally changed, if not eliminated entirely. To judge an organ's capacity, for example, by its forced response to a question about shapes in an inkblot is ludicrous when it is realized that the same organ can create multidimensional, holographic, varicolored, original, and projected images without assistance. This ability, variously labeled as daydreaming, hallucinating, or madness, is either taken for granted or denigrated. But it takes little acuity to realize that any organ that can both create and observe its own creation, at one and the same time, is spectacularly formidable.

Similarly, measuring general aptitude with standard "intelligence quota" (IQ) tests is absurd. Rather than employing sterile tools which measure whether some people are more "interesting" and "able" than others, surely it is time that we evolved. It is now the moment to see man, woman, and the universe as they are: infinitely involved, infinitely fascinating, and worthy, not of categorization and division, but of understanding.

The Second Spore

At exactly the same time that Tony Buzan was editing the international Mensa journal and pondering on the significance of the information he had been gathering on the human brain, coauthor Raymond Keene at Trinity College, Cambridge, was studying European literature, language, history, and culture, and specifically that towering German genius, Johann Wolfgang von Goethe. Ray was struck by an apparently serious anomaly: he was constantly informed by members of the surrounding academic environment that the fires of creativity regularly "burn out" by the age of twenty-six. It was also commonly stated that chess players (and chess is Ray's second career) peak at twenty-six and then are "past it." "Thinking like a forty-year-old" is, in fact, a common term of disparagement among chess players.

Such commonplaces of academic wisdom, though, did not sit well with the awkward fact that the work of the chess champions, artists, writers, transcultural giants, and inspirational greats and geniuses whom Ray was studying frequently—rather than exceptionally—seemed to produce better work as they got older. In many cases, an artist's supreme creation, dwarfing all previous work, was his final piece, often brought to fruition in extreme old age.

All the great minds seemed to have a clear creative vision and purpose and strove toward its fulfillment with barely credible levels of determination and persistence.

Should anyone doubt this, then simply examine the chronologically ordered numbers that define when a particular masterpiece was written or composed. Who would deny that Beethoven's Ninth Symphony (and he only wrote nine) marked his creative peak? Who would deny that *Faust* part 2 (and there are only two parts) is Goethe's deepest and richest work? The list goes on. . . . Shakespeare's late plays, in particular *The Tempest* (his last), are his most magical; Leonardo da Vinci started painting the *Mona Lisa* when he was fifty-two; Michelangelo began work as papal architect-in-chief on St. Peter's in Rome at the age of sixty-three; Brahms' Fourth Symphony (he only wrote four), composed when he was fifty-one, exceeds all his previous compositions in its grandeur of structure, opulence of melody, harmony, and tonality. Brahms, in fact, only turned his hand to writing symphonies at all when he was forty-three (Symphony Number 1). Sinan, the imperial architect of the Constantinople (today's Istanbul) of the Ottoman sultans, created his crowning glory, the Edirne Mosque, when in his eighties.

Obviously some serious misconceptions were collectively, if subconsciously, developing. Academics were telling their students one thing but were lecturing about works that refuted their own predictions. This phenomenon required both investigation and questioning.

The Third Spore

The third major event took place in April 1986, when an organization called Turning Point asked Tony Buzan to address its monthly meeting in Stockholm. As its name suggests, Turning Point had been formed by a group of minds who felt that humankind, and indeed the entire planet, was at a turning point. Both as individuals and as a group, they needed to acquire as much information as possible to help them make a positive contribution to the future of the human race. During his lecture on the brain, Tony distributed a questionnaire. This asked the group's members to rate themselves on a scale of 0–100 in various categories, including learning skills, intelligence, general self-evaluation, and hope for the future.

The average rating in each category was between 60 and 70.

This was definitely above average, but far below what might be expected in a group that had come together specifically because it believed in the future and believed it could contribute to it.

As Tony continued to discuss the brain and the future, he was simultaneously exploring the question, "What can one do to help individuals such as these (and indeed all individuals and groups), long past the stage of standard formal learning, to develop their phenomenal natural capacities in a way that is both continually self-regenerating and expansive?" Learning, thinking, and self-improvement certainly do not cease at the end of one's formal education.

The Good News

As a result of these extraordinary confluences, the authors independently and together gathered data about what a human being *really* is, and what, therefore, its potential could be.

Aging Agelessly is the answer for those who want their brains and mental performance to continuously surge forward. This book is for anyone who wishes to gain access to their brain and wishes to use it well for the whole of their life and at any age, from eight to eighty, and beyond!

Research is increasingly proving that the creative and memory powers of the brain tend toward the infinite—and, far from declining, can actually increase as you age. We plan now to tell you how.

What Should I Do Now?

First, read the next chapter to determine your estimated life expectancy. Then you can set about extending it and maximizing the quality of time available to you.

Brain Flash
On the Brain Beat

No superlative, it seems, is too grand to explain what is happening to brain research. . . . Gerald Fischback, Professor of Neurobiology at Harvard, believes philosophers enquiring into the human condition can no longer ignore the brain experiments that are "among the most urgent, challenging and exciting" in all of science. "Our survival, and probably the survival of this planet, depends on a more complete understanding of the human mind," he says.

The brain weighs about the same as a bag of sugar—about 2 percent of body weight—but accounts for up to 20 percent of the body's energy needs.

A million million nerve cells are packed into every human head. There are as many stars in the Milky Way galaxy as there are cells between your ears.

Each nerve cell can be connected with up to 100,000 others. Counting each nerve connection in the human brain cortex—the outer layer—at the rate of one a second would take 32 million years.

As each connection involves at least 50 different chemical transmitters, *the human brain is the most complex structure known to the human mind.*

Plato, the Greek philosopher who was born in 428 BC, was the first to conclude, correctly, that the brain was the "originating power of the perceptions and hearing and sight and smell."

—The Independent on Sunday Review

CHAPTER 2

Exploring and Estimating Longevity

*And the LORD said, my spirit shall not always strive
with man, for that he also is flesh: yet his days
shall be an hundred and twenty years.*

—Genesis 6:3

This chapter is a call to arms and a challenge to prevailing misconceptions about age. You will be introduced to the extraordinary realities of what has been achieved in terms of human longevity. And we provide a benchmark test that allows you to calculate your own predicted life expectancy and shows you how to adjust it appropriately—down or up—based on numerous factors!

The Lineage of Confucius
The lineage of the celebrated Chinese philosopher K'ung Fu-tzu, more famously known as Confucius (551–479 BC), can be traced back further than that of any other family. His great-,

great-, great-, great-grandfather K'ung Chia is known from the eighth century BC, while Confucius's 80th-generation mainline descendent, Kung Yu-jen, was born in 2006 in Taipei, keeping the 2,500-year lineage of the First Sage alive in twenty-first century Taiwan.

Individual Longevity

Based on United Nations estimates, the world was home to nearly half a million centenarians (people aged 100 and older) in 2015, more than four times as many as in 1990. This growth is expected to accelerate, with the total increasing to 3.7 million centenarians by the year 2050. The share of children younger than 15 is expected to drop from 26.6 percent in 2010 to 21.3 percent in 2050, while the share of people aged 65 and older is expected to double, from 7.7 percent in 2010 to 15.6 percent in 2050.

Distribution of the Global Population by Age, 1950, 2010, and 2050

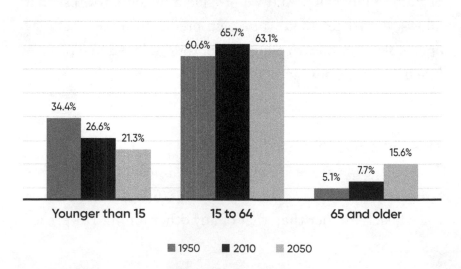

The US leads the world in respect to the overall number of centenarians, with 72,000, followed by Japan, China, India, and Italy. However, Japan leads the world in the number of persons 100 and older per 10,000 people, with 4.8 centenarians per 10,000 people, followed by Italy (with 4.1), the US (with 2.2), China (with 0.3), and India (with 0.2).

According to a relatively recent report entitled *An Aging World: 2015*, commissioned by the National Institute on Aging (NIA), part of the National Institutes of Health (NIH), and produced by the US Census Bureau, 8.5 percent of people worldwide (617 million) are aged 65 and over, and this percentage is projected to double to nearly 17 percent of the world's population by 2050. Here are some highlights from the report:

- America's 65-and-over population is projected to nearly double over the next three decades, from 48 million to 88 million by 2050.
- By 2050, global life expectancy at birth is projected to increase by almost 8 years, climbing from 68.6 years in 2015 to 76.2 years in 2050.
- The global population of the "oldest old"—people aged 80 and older—is expected to more than triple between 2015 and 2050, growing from 126.5 million to 446.6 million. The oldest old population in some Asian and Latin American countries is predicted to quadruple by 2050.
- Among the older population worldwide, noncommunicable diseases are the main health concern. In low-income countries, many in Africa, the older population faces a considerable burden from both noncommunicable and communicable diseases.

- Risk factors—such as tobacco and alcohol use, insufficient consumption of vegetables and fruit, and low levels of physical activity—contribute directly or indirectly to the global burden of disease. Changes in risk factors have been observed, such as a decline in tobacco use in some high-income countries. The majority of smokers worldwide now live in low- and middle-income countries.

As life expectancy increases, the importance of aging well will only increase. While longevity is certainly admirable, the goal isn't focused solely on years lived but also on the quality of the life lived.

The Oldest Person Ever

The greatest authenticated age to which any human has ever lived was 122 years, 164 days, by Jeanne Louise Calment of France. She was born on February 21, 1875—approximately fourteen years before the Eiffel Tower was built and fifteen years before motion pictures were invented. The year after her birth, Tolstoy published *Anna Karenina* and Alexander Graham Bell patented the telephone. She once met Vincent Van Gogh (who died on July 29, 1890) in her father's shop.

Some of her close family members also exhibited longevity; her brother lived to the age of ninety-seven, her father to ninety-three, and her mother to eighty-six.

The World's Longest-Lived People

Rank	Country	Years	Name	Born	Died
1	France	122	Jeanne Louise Calment	2/21/1875	8/4/1997
2	Japan	120	Shigechiyo Izumi	6/29/1865	2/21/1986
3	USA	119	Sarah Knauss	9/24/1880	12/30/1999
4	Japan	119	Kane Tanaka	1/2/1903	4/19/2022
5	France	118	Lucile Randon	2/11/1904	1/27/2023
6	Japan	117	Nabi Tajima	8/4/1900	4/21/2018
7	Canada	117	Marie-Louise Meilleur	8/29/1880	4/16/1998
8	Jamaica	117	Violet Brown	3/10/1900	9/15/2017
9	Japan	117	Chiyo Miyako	5/21/1901	7/22/2018
10	Japan	117	Misao Okawa	3/5/1898	4/1/2015

Amazing Age Facts

Human beings are not the only living things with astonishing longevity records. The oldest continuously living things in the world are plants. Pando, the name of a massive clonal colony of quaking aspens in Utah's Fishlake National Forest, is estimated to be over 80,000 years old.

The oldest living tree in the world is a Californian bristlecone pine named Methuselah, which is over 4,800 years old and still going strong! This tree was alive when Homer composed the *Iliad,* when Buddha preached nirvana, and when Christ gave the Sermon on the Mount.

The oldest *revived* living entities in the world are bacterial spores lying dormant inside a fossil bee, which suddenly surged back to life after 40 million years. This feat of resurrection was achieved by microbiologists Raúl Cano and Monica Borucki of California Polytechnic State University at San Luis Obispo. Their work was carried out in early 1995 and involved releasing small stingless bees from fossilized tree sap (amber).

But the Immortal Jellyfish even has that beat; they never die—they just sink to the ocean floor and start their lifecycle all over again.

The Longevity Quiz:
Estimate Your Own Life Expectancy

Diana S. Woodruff-Pak is a psychologist who believes that we all have the capacity to live to 100. In fact, biologists now set the upper limit for human life even higher—maybe as high as 125. Indeed, they are in excellent company. Although the biblically sanctioned lifespan is normally said to be "three score years and ten" (= 70; Psalm 90:10), Genesis suggests that the human lifespan "shall be an hundred and twenty years" (Genesis 6:3). After years of research on longevity, we have drawn up the quiz that follows, which enables you to estimate how long you will live. Our own view is that intellectually and physically active, contented fun lovers have the best chance of living to be 100 or more.

Start by looking up your present age in the table. Against this, you will find your basic life expectancy, derived from figures produced by insurance actuaries. Then, answering the questions on the following pages, add to or subtract from this figure, according to how your own lifestyle and personality are likely to affect your longevity.

Women can expect to live roughly three years longer than men (on whom this table is based). Women should therefore add three years to the basic life expectancy presented in the chart.

Basic Life Expectancy Chart

Present Age	Est. life expectancy	Present Age	Est. life expectancy	Present Age	Est. life expectancy
15	70.7	39	72.4	63	77.3
16	70.8	40	72.5	64	77.7
17	70.8	41	72.6	65	78.1
18	70.8	42	72.7	66	78.4
19	70.9	43	72.8	67	78.9
20	71.1	44	72.9	68	79.3
21	71.1	45	73.0	69	79.7
22	71.2	46	73.2	70	80.2
23	71.3	47	73.3	71	80.7
24	71.3	48	73.5	72	81.2
25	71.4	49	73.6	73	81.7
26	71.5	50	73.8	74	82.2
27	71.6	51	74.0	75	82.8
28	71.6	52	74.2	76	83.3
29	71.7	53	74.4	77	83.9
30	71.8	54	74.7	78	84.5
31	71.8	55	74.9	79	85.1
32	71.9	56	75.1	80	85.7
33	72.0	57	75.4	81	86.3
34	72.0	58	75.5	82	87.0
35	72.1	59	76.0	83	87.6
36	72.2	60	76.3	84	88.2
37	72.2	61	76.6		
38	72.3	62	77.0		

Calculate Your Own Life Expectancy

1. Add one year for each of your grandparents who lived to be 80 or more or is 80 and still alive. Add half a year for each one who topped 70 or is 70 and still alive.

2. Add 4 years if your mother lived beyond 80 and two years if your father did as well. Do the same for living parents who have reached these ages.

3. Subtract 4 years if any sister, brother, parent, or grandparent died of a heart attack, stroke, or arteriosclerosis before the age of 50. Subtract 2 years for each of these who died between 50 and 60.

4. Subtract 3 years for each sister, brother, parent, or grandparent who died of diabetes mellitus or peptic ulcer before 60. If any of these died of stomach cancer before then, subtract 2 years. For any other illnesses that killed them before 60 (except those caused by accidents), subtract 1 year.

5. Women who cannot have children, or plan none, subtract half a year. Women with over 7 children, subtract 1 year.

6. If you are a first-born, add 1 year.

7. Add 2 years if your intelligence is above average (i.e., if you have an IQ of over 100).

8. Smoking: If you smoke fewer than 20 cigarettes per day, subtract 2 years; if 20–40 cigarettes, subtract 7 years; if you smoke more than 40 cigarettes a day, subtract 12 years.

9. If you enjoy regular sex once or twice a week, add 2 years.

10. If you have a thorough annual checkup, add 2 years.

11. If you are overweight (or ever have been), subtract 2 years.

12. If you sleep more than 10 hours every night, or less than 5 hours a night, subtract 2 years.

13. Drinking: one or two whiskies, one pint/half a liter of wine, or up to a maximum of four glasses of beer per day, counts as moderate: add three years. If you don't drink every day, add only one and a half years. If you don't drink at all, don't add or subtract anything. Heavy drinkers and alcoholics—subtract 8 years.

14. Exercise: For 3 times a week—jogging, cycling, swimming, brisk walks, dancing, skating, etc.—add 3 years. Weekend walks don't count.

15. Do you prefer simple, plain foods, vegetables, and fruit over richer, meatier, fatty foods? If you can say yes honestly, and you stop eating before you are full, add 1 year.

16. If you are frequently ill, subtract 5 years.

17. Education: if you did postgraduate work at university, add 3 years. For an ordinary bachelor's degree, add 2. If you have a high-school diploma, add 1. If you did not finish high school, add zero.

18. Jobs: if you are a professional person, add 1½ years; technical, managerial, administrative, and agricultural workers, add 1 year; proprietors, clerks, and sales staff, add nothing; semiskilled workers, take off half a year; laborers, subtract 4 years.

19. If, however, you're not a laborer but your job involves a lot of physical work, add 2 years. If it is a desk job, subtract 2 years.

20. If you live in a metropolitan area, or have done so for most of your life, subtract 1 year. Add 1 year if most of your time has been spent in the countryside.

21. If you are married and living with your spouse, add 1 year. However, if you are a separated man living alone, subtract 9 years; 7 if you are a widower living alone. If you live with others, subtract only half these figures. Women who are separated or divorced, subtract 4 years; widows, 3½, unless you live with others, in which case subtract only 2.

22. If you have one or two close friends in whom you confide, add 1 year.

23. Add 2 years if you regularly play mind sports.

24. If your attitude to life is both positive and realistic, add 4 years.

Armed with this information, you can now calculate your own life expectancy. Remember to add 3 years if you are female.

The results of this quiz are a guide to your probable life expectancy if you continue your patterns of behavior as they are at present. The remainder of *Aging Agelessly* is designed to encourage you and guide you in various ways to increase your score (no matter what it is now) dramatically.

What Should I Do Now?

1. If you smoke, first cut down, then give up the habit entirely (see chapter 4).

2. Have a thorough annual medical checkup.

3. If you are over- or underweight, find the appropriate weight for you as an individual and work toward achieving it. Ask your doctor what your ideal weight should be.

4. If you drink heavily, cut down.

5. Take up regular exercise, particularly aerobic exercise, and aim to do it for at least twenty minutes three times weekly.

6. Take up mind sports, such as chess, bridge, or go.

You may think that you can't do all, or indeed any, of the above, but in chapter 4 we will show you how!

Brain Flash
The Drink Tank

Wine is the most healthful and hygienic of beverages.
—Louis Pasteur, French scientist

Drink no longer water but use a little wine for thy stomach's sake and thine often infirmities.
—1 Timothy 5:23

There are more old drunkards than old doctors.
—Benjamin Franklin

Red wine can be a part of your regular diet, as long as you do not drink excessively—no more than about half a liter a day.
—Michel Montignac, French dietitian

CHAPTER 3
Extending Your Life Expectancy

Had we but world enough and time.
—Andrew Marvell, "To His Coy Mistress"

In this chapter, we look at two different ways of staying vigorous and fit and extending your life expectancy—in other words, "manufacturing your own time." The first is hormone replacement therapy (HRT). Is it a good thing? We doubt it, but it may be worth researching on your own and deciding (with close consultation with your healthcare providers) whether it might be beneficial for you. We lean more in the direction of drawing on our own physical and mental resources to stay young and fit.

In this chapter, we list the top twenty areas of mental performance that require improvement among forty- to fifty-year-olds and show you how to improve in each of these areas. But first, we provide some background discussion about different approaches to stopping and turning back the clock.

Brain Flash
100 Going on 45!

Edward L. Bernays coined the term *public relations* in 1919 and is widely regarded as the father of public relations. When he turned 100, he said his mental age was "no different from when I was 45." He added, "When you reach 100, don't let it throw you, because "a person has many ages, and chronological is the least important."

Stopping the Clock . . . and Potentially Reversing It

"You can be as vibrant at sixty as you were at thirty!"

How often have you heard this claim, offering the elixir of eternal youthfulness? It is made increasingly by the purveyors of various hormone therapies (hormone replacement therapy and human growth hormones), who assert that the demonstrable benefits, to both men and women, of taking such substances include: higher energy levels; increased stamina; greater sex drive; retrieval of skin elasticity, normally associated with younger people; stronger bones; and more efficiently functioning hearts. Courses of testosterone, to cope with the male andropause, and of estrogen, to combat the female menopause, are the favored methods—and some claim the effect is miraculous.

Others accuse the purveyors of being nothing better than snake oil salesmen who are cynically medicalizing the normal aging process.

For example, an article in *Time* magazine does a fine job of highlighting the pros and cons of HRT for women:

Estrogen is indeed the closest thing in modern medicine to an elixir of youth—a drug that slows the ravages of time for women. It is already the Number 1 prescription drug in America, and it is about to hit its demographic sweet spot: the millions of baby-boomers, now experiencing their first hot flushes . . . but what today's women should know is that, like every other magic potion, this one has a dark side.

To gain the full benefits of estrogen, a woman must take it not only at menopause, but also for decades afterward. It means a lifetime of drug-taking and possible side-effects that include an increased risk of several forms of cancer . . . weighing such risks against the truly miraculous benefits of estrogen may be the most difficult health decision a woman can make:

Whether to take HRT in the form of estrogen or testosterone is clearly a matter for individual choice.

Take Control of Your Own Longevity and Physical and Cognitive Health

What we offer here is quite different. Our own strategy, as mapped out in this book, enables the reader to draw entirely on his or her untapped inner resources and strength. We do recommend a healthy diet and vitamins, not drugs, as well as aerobic exercise, but the main thrust of our argument is to show you how your mental performance can improve with age simply by harnessing the phenomenal power within your own personal biocomputer and by learning the truth about what can actually happen to your brain as you age.

Consider This

Your brain is a sleeping giant. Many experts believe that we use as little as 1 percent of our full potential.

Even though you have conceivably spent between 1,000 and 10,000 hours formally learning history, languages, literature, mathematics, geography, and political science, you will probably, no matter what age you are now, have spent only a few hours specifically learning the following skills:
- Creative thinking
- Concentration—memory performance
- The relationship between brain function and aging
- The art of communication
- Comprehensive approaches to study and technical reading
- The effect of our modes of thought on habit patterns and change (metapositive thinking)

Concentration and Comprehension

Statistics show that, on average, executives, businesspeople, academics, and all professionals spend:
- Thirty percent of their professional time reading and sorting through information.
- Twenty percent of their time solving problems and thinking creatively.
- Twenty percent of their time communicating.

It is therefore essential that these skills be learned by *everyone* and that the brain be trained accordingly.

Benefits

The strategy outlined in this book will give you the techniques and the knowledge to become more effective, and a much better thinker and communicator, as you progress through life. You will be able to:

- Remember names, facts, and figures using memory techniques that are easy to learn and master.
- Achieve higher levels of creativity, clearer organization of your thoughts, increased concentration and more concise communications through the introduction and use of Mind Mapping. This is a technique for accessing your range of intelligence, improving all your thinking skills, and dramatically improving your memory and creativity.
- Read more rapidly and assimilate all the materials you need to.
- Gain greater insights into your own potential by learning from the principles and techniques used by great minds in the business, sports, and creative worlds. You will be shown ways of applying these principles to improve your own potential for greater success.

With this knowledge, you will be able to achieve just about anything you set out to achieve and do it progressively better as you mature!

Learn How to Learn at Any Age

Aging Agelessly is designed to assist you in the next leap in evolution: the self-awareness of intelligence and the knowledge that this intelligence too can be nurtured, starting at any time and at any age, to astounding advantage. Consider the following:

- Stock market analysts watch, like hawks, ten individuals in California's Silicon Valley. When there is even a hint that one of them might move from Company A to Company B, the world's stock markets shift.

- According to the Association for Talent Development, companies that offer comprehensive training programs have 218 percent higher income per employee than companies without formalized training. They also have a 24 percent higher profit margin.

- According to a report released by the National Bureau of Economic Research (NBER), improved math skills lead to a 28 percent increase in wages, while improved reading skills in education would result in a 27 percent boost in wages.

- The primary economy among developed nations isn't based so much on manufacturing as it is on knowledge—human capital and intangible assets, such as proprietary technology. The most valued skill sets in the knowledge economy are driven by brainpower—creating and working with algorithms, data analysis, data-based decision making, and innovation.

- In the armed forces of an increasing number of countries, mental martial arts have become as important as physical combat skills.

- National Olympic squads devote as much as 30 percent of their training time to the development of mindset, stamina, and visualization skills.

- According to *Training* magazine's *2021 Training Industry Report*, "US training expenditures rose nearly 12 percent to $92.3 billion in 2020–2021."

The Top Twenty Areas of Mental Performance Requiring Improvement among Forty- to Fifty-Year-Olds

Let us now consider this encouraging news in a different context. Many people in their forties and fifties are anxious to improve their mental performance and powers but face difficulty in achieving their goals. The following pages take you on a quick guided tour of the problems that people increasingly face as they get older. These are the main areas we suggest you focus on in developing your own intellectual capital as you age. Many of the themes touched upon here will be developed and expanded in later chapters.

Over the past twenty years, we have polled more than 100,000 people on each of the five continents. Among the more than one hundred mental skill areas commonly mentioned as requiring improvement, here are the top twenty:

1. Memory
2. Concentration
3. Presentation skills, public speaking
4. Written presentation skills
5. Creative thinking
6. Planning
7. Thought organization
8. Problem analysis
9. Problem-solving

10. Motivation
11. Analytical thinking
12. Prioritizing
13. Reading speed (volume of material)
14. Reading comprehension
15. Time management
16. Dealing with stress
17. Dealing with fatigue
18. Assimilation of information
19. Time management: avoiding procrastination or time wasting
20. Decline of mental ability with age

With the aid of modern research into brain functioning, each area can be tackled with relative ease. We shall now touch on seven major topics that impinge on all of the above problems:

1. Left- and right-brain research
2. Mind Mapping
3. Speed-reading
4. Mnemonic techniques
5. Memory loss after learning
6. The brain cell—and, most importantly . . .
7. "Decline" of mental abilities with age

We shall relate each of these topics to the major problem areas and show how to apply your new knowledge to improve mental performance.

1. Left- and right-brain research.

It has now become common knowledge that the left and right hemispheres of the brain deal with different intellectual functions. The left cortex primarily handles logic, language, number, sequence, analysis, and listing; the right deals with rhythm, dimension, color, imagination, daydreaming, and spatial relationships.

It has only recently been realized that the left cortex is not the so-called academic side, nor is the right cortex the so-called creative, intuitive, emotional side. We now know, from extensive research, that the two hemispheres need to be used in conjunction for both academic and creative success.

The Einsteins, Newtons, Goethes, and Shakespeares of this world, like the great business geniuses, combined their linguistic, numerical, and analytical skills with their powers of imagination to produce their creative masterpieces.

Using this basic knowledge of brain functioning, we can train ourselves in skills relating to each of the problem areas, often producing improvements of as much as 500 percent.

Tony Buzan's key contribution to achieving such improvement is the Mind Map.

2. Mind Mapping.

In traditional note-taking—whether it be for memory, preparing communication, organizing thought, problem analysis, planning, or creative thinking—the standard mode of depiction is black-and-white, linear: sentences, short phrase lists, or numerically and alphabetically ordered lists. These methods lack color, visual rhythm, dimensions, images, and spatial relationships. As a result, they cauterize the brain's thinking capacities and are counterproductive to the aforementioned processes.

Mind Mapping (see chapter 9 for further details) uses the full range of your brain's abilities, placing a colorful image in the center of the page to facilitate memorization and the creative generation of ideas, and subsequently branching out in associative networks that externally mirror the brain's internal structures. The Mind Map can encapsulate a mass of information within a very small space. It can be used for both previewing and reviewing purposes.

By using Mind Maps, the preparation of speeches can be reduced in time from days to minutes; problems can be solved more rapidly; memory can be improved from failing to perfect; and creative thinkers can generate a limitless number of ideas rather than a short list. This is especially valuable if you feel that your memory and mental faculties are fading with age. The Mind Map is the perfect antidote.

3. Speed-reading.

It is possible to combine Mind Mapping with the new speed-reading techniques, which enable people to reach speeds of more than 1,000 words a minute, with excellent comprehension. The faster you can assimilate information, the more you can stimulate your brain and expand your horizons. Individuals, especially in companies, who can train themselves to do this can then form intellectual commando units, as described below. Speed-reading may sound difficult and esoteric, but it is quite easy to start.

Try this simple test, for instance. Time yourself reading a page of this book. Now read another page and time yourself again, but also do the following:

- Use a pointer to help you focus. You were possibly told not to do this at school. If so, you were told wrong!
- Follow your pointer and only go forward. Do not backslide or reread segments.
- Take in two words at a time, where before you took in one. This tactic alone will probably double your reading speed.

4. Forming intellectual commando units.

By reading at more advanced speeds, Mind Mapping in detail the outline of a book and its chapters, and exchanging the information gathered by using advanced Mind Mapping and presentation skills, an individual can acquire, integrate, memorize, and begin to apply an entire book's worth of new information in just one day. The implications for a company, or a number of its employees doing likewise simultaneously, are obvious.

5. Mnemonic techniques.

Mnemonics is the art of assisting memory by using a device such as a rhyme: for example, "Thirty days hath September, April, June, and November" makes it easy to remember the number of days in the months.

Mnemonic techniques were invented by the Greeks and were, until quite recently, dismissed as tricks. We now realize that these devices are soundly based on the brain's functioning. When applied appropriately, they can dramatically improve memory and recall.

Mnemonics uses the principles of association and imagination, making dramatic, colorful, sensual, and consequently unforgettable images in your mind. The Mind Map is a superb multidimensional mnemonic, using the brain's innate functional areas effectively to imprint the required information. You can start by remembering the people you meet at parties by associating their names with something distinctive about their appearance.

Using mnemonics, businesspeople have been trained to remember perfectly forty newly introduced people and memorize lists of over one hundred products, facts, and data. These techniques are now being applied at the IBM training center in Stockholm and have been a major reason for the success of its introductory training program.

6. Memory loss after learning.

This is a dramatic problem. After a one-hour learning period, there is a short rise in the recall of information as the brain integrates the new data. This is followed by a dramatic decline. By the end of twenty-four hours, as much as 80 percent of the detail has been lost.

The individual often confuses this effect with the decline of mental abilities with age. The truth is that the loss of recall ability is entirely due to standard recall curves. It should in no way be confused with age. With appropriate training, as we shall indicate, memory can actually improve with age.

The implications of these facts and misconceptions are disturbing, especially for business. Say a multinational firm spends $50 million a year on training. Within a few days, $40 million worth of that training will have been lost. However, by understanding the memory's rhythms, it is possible to avert this loss.

7. The brain cell.

In the last five years the brain cell has become the new frontier in the human search for knowledge. We have discovered that not only do we each have about 86 billion neurons, but that the interconnections between them can form patterns and memory traces that combine to give a number that is functionally equivalent to infinite.

Your brain, in just one second, can grasp concepts that it would take a mainframe supercomputer, operating at 400 million calculations per second, 100 years to accomplish. Clearly we have an inherent capacity to integrate and juggle multiple billions of bits of data. It has, therefore, become increasingly apparent to those involved in brain research that adequate training of the phenomenal biocomputer that each of us possesses will enormously accelerate and increase our ability to problem-solve, prioritize, create, and communicate.

Training, or (to put it more excitingly) challenging and stimulating the brain, is not solely the prerogative of young trainees. You can start at any age. The more you learn, the easier it is to learn more, and the more your brain builds both mental and physical associational networks, making it increasingly easy to access and manipulate data.

8. "Decline" of mental abilities with age.

The usual response to the question: "What happens to your brain cells as they get older?" is: "They die." But one of the most delightful pieces of news from the brain research front comes from Marion Diamond of the University of California, who has recently confirmed that in normal, active, and healthy brains, there is no brain cell loss with age. On the contrary, research now indicates that if the brain is used and trained, its interconnective complexity increases: intelligence is raised.

The Intelligence Revolution

We are at the beginning of a revolution, the like of which the world has never seen before: a huge leap in the development of human intelligence. In education, in business, and on the personal front, information from the psychological, neuro-physiological, and educational laboratories is being mobilized to dispel problems that had hitherto been accepted as part of the human aging process.

By applying our knowledge of the brain's separate functions, by externally representing our internal mental processes in Mind Map form, by making use of the innate elements and rhythms of memory, and by applying our new-found knowledge of the brain cell and the possibilities for continued improvement throughout our lives, a massive leap in evolution is not only possible but is happening. This book is in the vanguard.

Welcome, then, to the next great human adventure. An adventure in the exploration of your own vast and growing intelligences that should be expanding throughout life. An adventure that will prove stimulating, challenging, and profound. That adventure is you.

> ## Brain Flash
> ## Sinan
>
> Mimar Sinan (1491–1588), the imperial architect of the Ottoman sultan Suleiman the Magnificent, was first appointed to his job at the age of forty-seven. During his remaining fifty years, he designed and completed no fewer than 500 buildings, including palaces, tombs, hospitals, schools, and public baths, as well as the greatest mosques in the Ottoman Empire. Sinan saw the dimensions and architectural brilliance of the Christian church Hagia Sophia in Istanbul (like the Parthenon in Athens, a monument to "Divine Intelligence") as his lifelong challenge. He finally achieved his ambition to equal its beauty and surpass its size in his eighties, with the completion of his Selimiye Mosque at Edirne. He wrote proudly in his memoirs: "Christians say that they have defeated the Muslims, because no dome has been built in the Islamic world which can rival the dome of Hagia Sophia. I determined to create such a dome."

What Should I Do Now?

1. Remember this most important fact: the more you learn, the easier it is to learn more!
2. Learn how to speed-read using the tips given in this chapter. If you read at a faster rate, you can acquire information more readily and expand your horizons.
3. Try to improve your memory. Start with the names of people you meet at parties. Look for something distinctive in their appearance or at what they are wearing, so that you can lock their name onto it. Use mnemonic techniques to help you remember the names.

4. Look at questions and problems from all sides. *Think flexible*. Try new solutions and experiences, as these will help you retain your mental alertness.
5. Become socially involved. Degeneration occurs faster among older people who withdraw from an active social life. Meet people. Try to solve their problems!

CHAPTER 4

The Methuselah Mandate:

Achieving Your Full Potential (However Long It Takes)

Miss not the discourse of the elders.
—SIRACH 8:9

In previous chapters, we discovered that there are tools and methodologies for improving your various intelligences. In this chapter, we take you to the core of our argument. We reveal the ultimate good news: your brain is a flexible, organic, constantly changing, and (hopefully) constantly growing organ. As we progress through life, it can continue to become increasingly complex, more sophisticated, more elegant, and more useful to its owner. It will do so if you apply the guidance presented in this book.

Your ability to transform harmful habits and attitudes to take on new modes of behavior is vital to improved performance as you age. It's never too late to start, and *now* is the time to begin.

Brain Cells and Metapositive Thinking:
The Power to Change Yourself for the Better

In the pages that follow, we shall discuss a subject of increasing global interest and importance: what actually happens to the human brain as it progresses through the decades of its existence.

We will supply evidence for the case we are making: that, with appropriate training, most of the standard delusions about the brain can be laid to rest and a new awareness of what actually does happen can be initiated—a complete revolution in learning.

According to the Bible, Methuselah was the oldest known human (in Genesis it is said that he lived for 969 years). The Methuselah mandate is a call for all humans to achieve the full realization of their potential throughout life.

It is interesting to study memory, brain cells, creativity, and so on, but arguably studying all those in the context of their progression through life is most fascinating of all. What we would like to do, first of all, is show you the standard graph depicting what many people mistakenly believe happens to the brain as it gets older.

The vertical axis represents intellectual capacity—or skills—and the horizontal axis represents time. Standard graphs on intelligence published by psychologists such as Hans Eysenck (which you will find in most introductory psychological texts) show a phenomenal early growth in intellectual skills. This reaches a peak between the late teens and early twenties. Researchers usually go on to cite vast amounts of evidence to support this, including stories about the great

Mental Abilities/Age

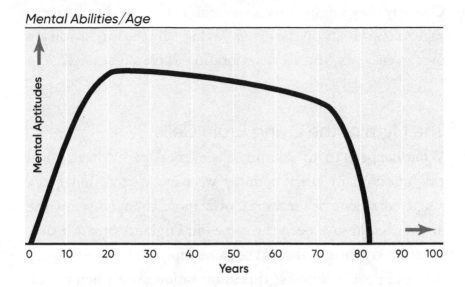

mathematicians and how, throughout history, without exception, they have never done any great original work after the age of twenty-six.

IQ tests generally confirm this claim, and studies by people reporting on themselves show that they think their memories definitely deteriorate with age. In other words, their experience of their own mental processes as they age is that of diminishing.

There is also the physical correlation: after the age of twenty-six, the body's physical skills tend to decline. Since brain cells are part of the body, they must be deteriorating as well. There is then a steady process of degeneration, with a rapid decline near the end. Not a very rosy picture.

It is worth thinking about this: Assume that extraterrestrial beings exist, and they've decided to invade our planet. They know that humans are highly motivated and resourceful, so they want to devise an effective way to demotivate us.

One way they might consider would be to send down a message to everybody on the planet saying, "By the way, if you are over twenty-six, you are deteriorating. Have a nice day!"

The Myth of the Dying Brain Cells

What happens to your brain cells every day? We have asked this question in every country we have visited. On every single continent of the world, over more than 20 years, the answer has always been the same—in England, New Mexico, Taiwan, Argentina, always the same reply: "They die!" Every group of people "knows" this information. And when we ask how many brain cells die each day, again the reply comes with certainty, and almost with delight: "About a million!" What impact do you think this has on the planet?

Imagine waking up. The sun is shining, the birds are singing, your true love is by your side, and you look on the pillow—and there are a million dead brain cells. Those brain cells are your computer chips, and you have just lost another million. Every day you lose a million more. Whether you think about it or not, you are doomed!

You cannot be fundamentally optimistic if you believe that your entire operating system is falling apart. This is why, as people get older, they get very frightened of the "young stallions." Why? Because young people have more brain cells; they have more powerful biocomputers. If you are trying to compete with them, you are obviously going to lose unless you can manage to hold on to what you have got—and hold—and hold—until you have only about ten brain cells left, and then you let go.

Begin to think about the attitude instilled in the global population by such a self-defeating belief. It is devastatingly serious. It is like a case of intellectual Alzheimer's disease, which actually gets in and erodes intelligence. It dominates and destroys. Imagine if *Jeopardy!* champion Brad Rutter, or the world chess champion, Magnus Carlsen, or a top conductor like Gustavo Dudamel were to live by this information. They would be trying to hang on to their titles and their creative drive, although every day they may be losing a million brain cells. What would this mean to them, assuming it were true?

Further evidence for this misplaced belief comes from our social structure. What do we do with old people? We retire them! Look at the unbelievable irony. Take Jean Buzan, Tony Buzan's mother. She earned a degree in gerontology at the age of fifty-seven, lectured at university for eight years, and then was told that, because she was over sixty-five, she was too old to lecture on the topic! Utter lunacy. We retire people at sixty-five because they are "mentally incompetent," yet at the same time we routinely leave politicians over sixty-five in power. It's worth investigating the logic behind these decisions.

We have retirement homes, where treatment providers are taught how to deal with old people. We regiment the elderly, tell them they are no longer sexual, give them inane things to do like basket weaving, and pat them on the head. We don't allow them to do things for themselves: they are too old, so they might not be able to. "Don't worry—we'll do it for you. Don't get up—we'll get it for you." We are killing them. A depressing and horrible picture.

Let's take this assumption apart and look at the evidence. The first thing to look at is measured decline.

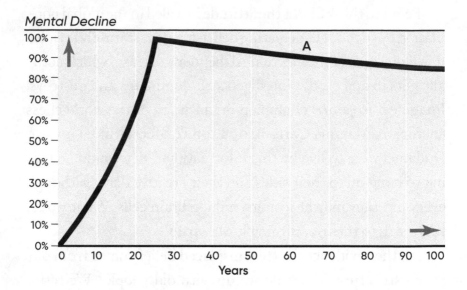

If you look at the straight line (marked A) in the chart, you will see that mental decline actually amounts to only 5–15 percent over an entire lifetime. So although it is steady, it is not steep. Nor is it new to old age. If you have woken up the morning after a fantastic party, you will have experienced your intellectual capacities working at a level of only about 2 percent—and that's at any age. So this is not a new experience.

What is interesting is just how staggeringly resilient the brain is. Look how we abuse it over a lifetime, and yet it declines only by 5–15 percent over the course of about 80 years. That's extraordinary.

The Outliers: Renegades from the Norm

The next thing to examine is the research on the supposed deterioration of the brain. It is a great statistical misunderstanding that the average statistic represents the average person. This just isn't true. The average statistic is made up of those who are above average as well as those who are below. In fact, some people's brains show a phenomenally steep decline, while others' brains actually improve, as well as all the different variations in between.

Those who are above average are described as statistical anomalies or outliers, and they "mess up" the chart. We like to refer to these people as "renegades from the norm." If you try to find common characteristics among these positive "renegades," you do indeed find that they have almost iden-

---

Brain Flash
Amazing Women Athletes

The oldest female athlete to complete the full distance in a marathon was Gladys Burrill from the United States at the age of 92 years, 19 days, at the Honolulu Marathon in Hawaii.

At the time of this writing, Ágnes Keleti, who turned 101 on January 4, 2022, was the oldest living Olympic champion. She became interested in gymnastics shortly before World War II and quickly became a top gymnast until the war interrupted her career and forced the cancellation of the 1940 and 1944 Olympics.

She resumed gymnastics after the war and was set to compete at the 1948 London Olympics but couldn't because of a last-minute ankle injury. Four years later, she competed at the 1952 Helsinki Games at the age of thirty-one, winning a gold medal in the floor exercise, along with a silver and two bronze medals.

Later, Keleti worked as a demonstrator at the Faculty of Gymnastics of the Budapest School for Physical Culture. She was also an accomplished musician, playing the cello professionally.

tical personality profiles: They are all interested in learning. In life, they are all positive, optimistic and in balance. They are all active, physically, mentally, emotionally, sensually, and sexually. Most of them have a highly developed sense of humor. They all tend to teach. Most consider themselves wealthy. And there is a growing number of them.

The graph showing physical decline (below) looks similar to the graph of mental decline, except that it is more marked.

Physical Decline

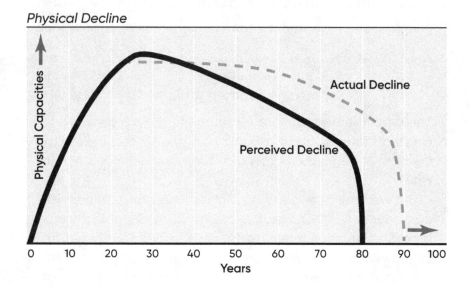

Here too the same misconceptions are beginning to be exposed. In terms of strength, the latest information supports the view that if the body is trained in strength, it reaches its physical peak at around the age of fifty. If we look at stamina, we see that long-distance marathon swimmers are usually in the thirty age range. So the physical graph is changing. We don't know yet exactly when physical strength begins to decline, but the rate is much less steep than was previously thought. There are now competitions called the Senior

Olympics, in which athletes in their fifties and up compete in twenty different sports, including basketball, cycling, soccer, swimming, track and field, and the triathalon. It's not unusual to see athletes in their eighties competing and performing quite well.

An Evolutionary Hiccup

Evidence now indicates that—physically, cardiovascularly, muscularly, and with regard to flexibility—not much changes in the body as it ages as long as it is kept healthy. On the physical side, we begin to see that biased thinking has crafted false impressions. With the brain, this is even more true. And the "renegades from the norm" suggest that everyone can follow their example. Maybe the degeneration was just an evolutionary stage, a hiccup in time, when the brain was nurtured in such a way that drove its decline. The actual evidence fails to support many of the overly pessimistic perceptions. It does not show that the brain gets worse with age. It shows that the human brain—under the right conditions—continues to improve.

Exaggerated Rumors

Let's move on to the widespread reports about declining memory. They turn out to be the result of introspection based on a false piece of knowledge. There is a global society called the "my memory is getting worse as I am getting older" club, and you hear people congratulating each other, and empathizing with each other, about how bad their memories are. And that's at thirty years old!

Brain Flash
Your Brain: A Powerful Computer

Recent research suggests that stimulating the mind with mental exercise may cause brain cells, called neurons, to branch wildly. The branching causes millions of additional connections, or synapses, between brain cells. "Think of it," says Arnold Scheibel, Director of UCLA's Brain Research Institute, "as a computer with a bigger memory board. You can do more things more quickly!"

The capacity of the brain to change offers new hope for preventing and treating brain diseases. It helps explain why some people can:

- Delay the onset of Alzheimer Disease symptoms for years. Studies now show that the more educated a person is, the less likely he or she is to show symptoms of the disease. The reason: intellectual activity develops surplus brain tissue that compensates for tissue damaged by the disease.

- Make a better recovery from strokes. Research indicates that even when areas of the brain are permanently damaged by a stroke, new message routes can be created to get around the road block or to resume the function of that area.

David Snowdon of the Sanders-Brown Center on Aging at the University of Kentucky has found that those who earn college degrees, who teach, who constantly challenge their minds, live longer than the less educated. New thinking in brain science suggests that whether someone hits the wall at age 65 or at age 102 may be partly up to the individual.

—UCLA Brain Research Institute

Now if you actually want to check your memory and take a closer look at the great memory genius you used to be, go to any school at the end of the day and look at what is left behind by its young giants of learning and memory: pens, pencils, shoes, coats, and so on. The only difference between a six-year-old and a sixty-year-old is that when the 6-year-old gets home and realizes he's left his clothing or homework at school, he doesn't say to himself: "Oh, my God! I'm six years old, and my memory is going!"

By contrast, the adult builds up a belief in the perfect memory that he or she used to have while nurturing a belief about the failure of his or her current memory. The two build and feed on each other. That belief can bring down a mind. It could also bring down a race or a planet and could even extinguish intelligence.

So the reports can largely be eliminated as evidence, as they are manifestly delusions. They tie in with the experiments; the experiments tie in with the reports—and so on and on they go, hand in hand, in an ever-widening circle of despair.

The social evidence can be eliminated as well. Who says that we have to put sixty-five-year-olds into retirement? If you assume that the human race is 3 million years old, then the modern brain, with which we are all equipped, is only about 50,000 years old, which means that we have only a few generations' worth of experiments available to us. Not enough to condemn everyone over sixty-five to a life of misery.

We have the societal attitude that age is somehow bad, and the words that most people associate with it tend to be negative, patronizing, or sickeningly euphemistic.

Write down ten words that you think are most commonly connected with age. Some of the more common ones are:

- Sad
- Lonely
- Sick
- Old
- Poor
- Alone
- Dirty
- Crippled
- Slow
- Weak
- Pensioner
- Old-age pensioner
- Senior citizen

We want to put this into the context of a child. If a child grows up thinking these things about old age, what is he or she likely to do? Back away from it? Not think about it? What does such a belief do to the child? Just think about it for a minute.

The child won't want to see or think about old age; therefore it won't prepare for it. It will start to see all sorts of inadequacies in itself, because it is "getting older." That means that it will not be proactive toward age, because that would remind the child of the approaching horror. Now consider that as a global thought.

It is also a very recent state of mind, because it was not so long ago that such beliefs were *not* the norm. Write down the words that other societies gave to those people in their populations who were older—the oldest and wisest in their tribes.

Some of the words that we have collected in our research include:

- All-seeing
- Elder
- Guru
- Matriarch (female leader of a family)
- Oracle

- Oral historian
- Paterfamilias (male head of a family)
- Patriarch
- Revered
- Sage
- *Sensei* (Japanese for *mentor* or *teacher*)
- Venerable
- Veteran

Some of these terms of respect—and belief in them—still exist today among certain societies.

Lack of Proof

This leads us to the last "proof"—that brain cells are shed like dead skin over time. If these cells are the computer chips of the brain, then that's a pretty damning piece of evidence. We are pleased to report, however, that a few years ago, the *New Scientist* investigation team and the American researcher Marion Diamond both asked, "Who said that?" The evidence was supposed to be contained in a medical textbook. So they checked the references—and the references in those references—and it turned out, fundamentally, to be a giant circular argument.

Everybody was quoting everybody else—but there was no actual evidence, no real source. There were suggestions, implications, and hints, but there was no proof.

Researchers are now finding that the brain does *not* lose cells with age. In fact, when it thinks appropriately, each brain cell tends to grow *more* connection points. In other words, under a certain type of positive stress, the brain will generate a more sophisticated biocomputer, with more connection points and more potential as well as a greater ability to link bits of its knowledge together.

Brain Flash
The Aged Brain Is as Active as the Young Brain

A recent study of brain chemistry at the National Institute of Aging, using a brain scan to study men whose ages ranged from twenty-one to eighty-three, found that "the healthy aged brain is as active and efficient as the healthy young brain" based on the direct assessment of metabolic activity in various parts of the brain.

"What can happen," Dr. [Jerry] Avorn said, "is that an older person who is admitted to a hospital for something like a broken hip or heart attack can become confused as a side-effect of drugs or simply from the strangeness of the hospital routine. The condition is reversible, but the family, or even the physician, doesn't recognize that fact. They assume this is the beginning of senile dementia and pack the person off to a nursing home.

"No one knows what exact proportion of people in nursing homes needn't be there," he said, "but we have ample clinical evidence that the numbers are large."

—National Institute of Aging

So we are at a stage when we can actively disprove all the major items of hitherto accepted "evidence" for the brain's automatic degeneration with age.

We are investing hundreds of billions of pounds and dollars in the development of an intellectual system: a human being. But when it reaches its peak, at sixty-five, we say, "Cut the system off." This is so irrational as to be humorous. It also means that we are cutting off our collective memory, the history of our race. We are actually saying: "Your sixty-five or eighty-five years are completely irrelevant; they don't exist or have any meaning."

Companies are offering early retirement. Ironically, when a company does this, it loses its collective memory of how it handled a particular situation in the past, so it has lost its intellectual capital. When that situation occurs again, it has to hire back those who took early retirement as consultants! This book says, "Now is the time to change all that."

As the brain gets older, it must, of necessity, get better and better until the moment before it dies—as long as it is used well and with the right operating guide. Now we will show you how to do that.

The Brain Cell

The human brain has about 86 billion neurons. In mathematical terms, that is 86 times 10^9, or 86,000,000,000. To grasp the magnitude of that number, imagine building blocks. Every time you add a zero, you multiply the number of building blocks by 10.

Start with 10 as a pile of imaginary blocks in front of you. Add a zero. That multiplies the pile by 10, and now you have a pile of building blocks numbering 100 in front of you. Add another zero, and you multiply the blocks by 10 again. Now you have a pile of 1,000 blocks. One more zero, and 1,000 becomes 10,000. One more zero, and it becomes 100,000, and you just keep adding zeros until you have 1 followed by 9 zeros. Now imagine eighty-six of those piles of blocks. That's the number of neurons in the average human brain.

**Brain Flash
The Value of Experience**

Many organizations are going wrong because they have lost their collective "memory"—because somewhere in the business changes that have taken place in the last twenty years, the idea of experience has become devalued.

Experience is now viewed negatively, because it is said to hold back the speed of change within the organization.

Lack of experienced staff helps to explain the poor performance of one UK high-street bank. According to one academic, "By sacking long-serving managers every time they [the bank] made a business mistake, they wiped out the organizational memory and increased the chances of making further mistakes."

—Peter Herriot and Carole Pemberton,
Competitive Advantage through Diversity

Fiat Lux—Let There Be Light

The power of the brain cell is extraordinary. The more we have investigated it, the more we realize that the power is greater than we thought. One brain cell, genetically, holds in its memory the code for the perfect duplication of yourself. Think of the amount of information that it contains in order to do this. It's like a gigantic library, and that is only one tiny part of what it can do. It is considerably more powerful than any computer. One interesting fact: in your head there exists the potential for more human beings than there are on the planet. You contain a planet's worth of potential humans in your own head!

Tiny living beings, like bees, have identical brain cells to ours. The difference is that they have only a few thousand, yet look what they can do: they can smell, they can see, they can navigate, they can remember and communicate with each other. Research shows that insects like the bee have one brain cell that becomes like the godfather of the brain. It is no different from any of the others, but it is the boss. This shows the potential that lies within each cell. That's the power of the brain cell, and we have about 86 billion of them.

Each cell acts like a system on its own. It extends and seeks others to connect to. This seeking for connections is important. If you could see the brain, you would see the biggest cuddle circle in the world. Each brain cell wraps its tentacles around the others to create a package of interconnectivity. Along each tentacle are little "mushrooms" (like an octopus's sucker), and there are tens of thousands of these on each tentacle, and there are tens of thousands of tentacles, all connecting in millions of different ways. Inside each mushroom, on each tentacle, there are thousands of chemical formulae. Whenever you think, whatever you think, produces an electromagnetic, biochemical reaction. An impulse goes down one branch of one brain cell (for reasons we don't yet know and in ways we don't yet understand). Each brain cell is independent: each one makes its own decisions about where the message goes. Nevertheless, each cell is totally interdependent with the others. When a message comes down the tentacle and reaches the mushroom, a chemical cocktail is fired across the gap to the next mushroom on the next cell. This is called the *synaptic gap*.

So there is a pathway, which is known as a *memory trace*. It is an incredible, yet real, pattern of thought. It is a map of intellectual territory, it is a habit, and it is a probability. It is all these things at the same time, and it is real.

When the brain cell first starts to grow in a baby, it has a fundamental structure and growth. If a baby is not stimulated, the cells will simply tread intellectual water. They will not connect and grow of their own accord. Stimulation is the key food for growth of the organ and its complexity. It isn't the size of the cell that's important, but its interconnectivity and its sophistication.

The Limits of Learning

The question about the limits of human learning—the ability of the human to learn over time and through age—can be reduced, on one level, to a mathematical equation. How many brain cells are available? How many thoughts can the brain take in? Its limited capacity is often given as a reason for people to stop learning: "I am not going to learn any more: my brain is almost full, and I need to save the space." This kind of excuse is ludicrous.

So how many thought traces can we make? In the 1950s, the number of thought traces was calculated to be 10^{100}. After some time, this number was revised to 10^{800}. Even this was found to be too small. The number, calculated by the Russian neuroanatomist Pyotr Anokhin, is 1 followed by 6.5 million miles (10.5 million kilometers) of standard, 11-point typewritten zeros.

Our capacity is functionally limitless.

Metapositive Thinking:
The Power to Change Yourself for the Better

The thought process drives itself. So let's look at a thought in situ: in its natural state. Let's examine a brain cell and how it connects to other brain cells as a person develops a deeply engrained bad habit over time. This is a BBH, a Big Bad Habit, one that is counterproductive to your survival. You are aware of this habit and have decided to change it. Let's imagine that this habit involves eating two boxes of chocolates per day and that you weigh 400 pounds (181 kilograms) and have been doing this for 20 years.

What's the first thing that comes into your mind when you say: "I am not going to eat *chocolates*"? Notice the *first* thing that occurs to you when you even read that phrase—was it not the chocolates themselves? Did you see the packaging of your favorite ones? So a thought is whizzing through the circuits of your brain. It has run through many times before, because it is a habit, something you don't even think about: it is subconscious, and now you are trying to change it consciously. The good news is that even thinking, "I am going to change" actually does change the brain on a physiological level, causing different traces to activate through your brain cells.

But—and it's a big *but*—a habit is something you have been doing for years. Along comes a birthday and someone gives you chocolates. What are you thinking now as you look at the box?

Possibly "I'll just have one!"

This is a BBH, a Big Bad Habit; it took years to install it in your mental software, so you can't expect to change it all at once. But, bit by bit, every time you recommit to your goal, you can install new thought patterns and make new positive thoughts the GNH (Good New Habit).

Metapositive Thinking: The Key Steps

How do you do this? The best way is by deciding what to focus on and then by recommitting to it regularly. In the chocolate example, where was your focus? It was on the chocolates, wasn't it? So a more appropriate way of getting a handle on the subject would be to think about what you might gain by not eating chocolates. Your ultimate goal in conquering your Big Bad Habit and establishing a Good New Habit is to become fitter and healthier. How could we describe this goal? To be effective, an affirmation has to fulfill the following criteria:

- It must be personal: *I . . .*
- It must be stated in the present: *I am . . .*
- It must cover the process of what you are doing. This is important, because if you say to yourself, "I am healthy," and you aren't, you are actually lying to yourself, so: *I am becoming . . .*
- It must contain the goal within it: *I am becoming healthy.*

Recommitting to this goal regularly will help your brain rewire its BBH into a GNH. The illustration here shows the jaws of a Big Bad Habit and how your Good New Habits build up as you nurture their power. This is called *metapositive thinking,* or thinking for a change for the better.

The Metapositive Approach to Aging

How do these ideas apply to aging? Your thoughts about aging could be part of the BBH or the GNH. Which one would you like it to be? Most importantly in the context of designing strategies for successful aging, consider this. If you are trying to:

- Start doing aerobic exercise rowing, swimming, running, cycling), where previously you were doing none . . .
- Change or improve an unhealthy diet in order to improve your fitness and stamina . . .
- Give up smoking . . . or excessive drinking . . .
- Develop your powers of memory, take up a challenging new mental exercise, or develop a new mental skill, such as mind sports, chess, go, or Mind Mapping . . .
- Learn swimming or juggling or a martial art . . .

. . . then our message on the transformation of a Big Bad Habit into a Good New Habit is of central significance to you!

The Next Metapositive Step: TEFCAS

TEFCAS is a mnemonic devised by Tony Buzan to reflect how the brain learns and to help you remember this easily. To understand how TEFCAS works, let's take a concrete example. We teach go, chess, mind sports, and juggling at our seminars as a metaphor for learning. Juggling often strikes particular terror into the audience! When first confronted by the balls, many a stout-hearted individual has been seen to back away—even physically. The first throw may be successful or not—but how do you judge if it was successful if you have nothing to compare it with? You might look around and see how others are doing. If you are having limited success, you might give up quickly.

Your individual approach to learning, and how you process events, is the key to successful aging.

So how do you learn? Over the past ten years we have been collecting people's views from around the world, and they are generally the same. Illustrated below is the graphic representation of those views. It suggests that everyone learns and acquires new or changed habits in a smooth curve.

Standard Learning Graph

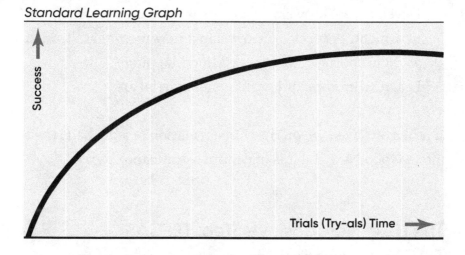

How completely wrong this illusion is! Yet it is extremely powerful and pervasive, in all cultures and all languages.
The brain has a very specific procedure for learning and for acquiring new skills, and we will use the TEFCAS mnemonic to spell it out:

T is for _trial_. You try something new: juggling, eating more healthily, cutting back on drinking, eliminating smoking, or starting aerobic exercise. Keeping interested and challenging your brain is part of trying something.

E is for _event_. Something happens. You catch the ball, or you don't. These are just events, not success or failure in and of themselves. If you divorce the emotion from the event, you can continue when others have "failed." It also means that you can apply clear criteria to what has happened, be it a "good" event or a "bad" one. You can learn from the data without the discouragement that results from judgment.

F is for _feedback_. How did you do? Getting appropriate feedback means that you will be able to assess accurately and plan your next stage.

C is for _check_. Check out your results against those of someone else—a professional, your teacher, or even your own goals.

A is for _adjust_. It was once said that the definition of madness was to keep doing something the same way while expecting a different result. So if what you are doing doesn't work, change your approach: try a different teacher or a different type of equipment, for example.

S is for _success_. Time for celebration. Reward the brain for success. Rewards engage the pleasure centers of your brain to reinforce learning and the effort that goes into it.

Es irrt der Mensch, so lang er strebt.

One errs for as long as one strives.

—JOHANN WOLFGANG VON GOETHE

This illustration shows how the brain learns, with its plateaus, troughs, and peaks. Next time you do something new, look at this chart to establish where you are in your learning. Do not be discouraged if you sometimes seem to be failing. This is normal and natural in the learning or changing process.

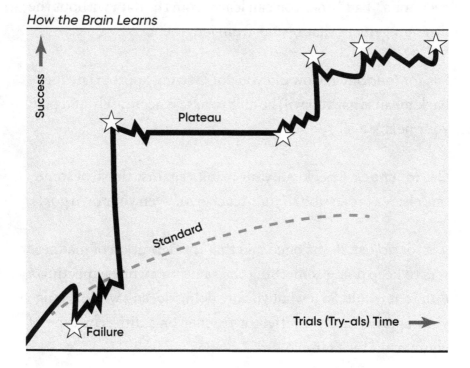

A Typical Metapositive Progression Using TEFCAS

Suppose that you are trying to quit smoking (a Big Bad Habit). Your metapositive progression using the TEFCAS model might go like this:

1. **Trial.** Constantly feeling below par.
2. **Event.** Smoking 40 cigarettes per day.
3. **Feedback.** Told by experts that this habit will reduce your life expectancy by 12 years.
4. **Check.** Go for a second opinion and advice.
5. **Adjust.** Gradually cut down on smoking. There will be peaks and troughs.
6. **Success.** Gradually—but steadily—become healthier.

Brain Flash
Nicotine Impairs Brain Cells

Contrary to earlier belief, research indicates that nicotine impairs, rather than stimulates, brain cells, which may explain the drug's calming effect, Linda Wong of the University of Texas at Galveston has stated. Wong claimed that nicotine appeared to suppress the rat brain cells that control basic behavior, such as learning, memory, and emotion. Her experiments and conclusions were presented at the 40th annual meeting of the American Society for Pharmacology and Experimental Therapeutics. They contradicted the traditional scientific belief that nicotine stimulates brain cells.

For years, scientists believed that the drug excites some neurons, which in turn inhibit other brain junctions to induce a calming effect on smokers. Wong said that her studies on rats suggested that nicotine directly reduces neuron activity in human beings. Her findings were based on a two-year study, in which nicotine was applied to tissue removed from the bases of rats' brains.

Wong was originally researching the mechanisms that control a neuron receptor linked to the theta rhythm (an electrical current produced by the brain). It was only by chance that she and her colleagues noticed that nicotine actually restrains neural activity. "It was startling and surprising," she said. She found that nicotine makes it more difficult to fire signals to other neurons, because the drug causes the affected neuron to release potassium, which critically inhibits the transmission of nervous impulses. Another explanation for the apparent "calming" effect of cigarettes in some smokers is that each time they inhale, they may be suffering a "minifaint" due to momentary lack of oxygen to the lungs and brain.

These findings are entirely in line with our life expectancy calculations in chapter 2, where we gave this clear warning:

Take off twelve years from your standard life expectancy if you smoke more than forty cigarettes a day.

The Metapositive Message:
It's Never Too Late (or Too Early) to Start

Learn everything! Later you will see
that nothing is superfluous.
—Hugh of St. Victor, twelfth century

Everything connects to everything else.
—Leonardo da Vinci

You now are armed with such phenomenal new information that it is possible for you to *expand your own brain!*

It is time to begin.

Brainstorm: Golden Rules

1. Believe in your brain and its capacity.
2. Study your brain at every level, from its biophysiology and neurochemistry to its huge range of mental skills. Understand both metapositive thinking and TEFCAS.
3. Cherish your brain.
4. Use it. As Leonardo da Vinci said in his own laws for developing a "complete" brain:
   - Study the science of art.
   - Study the art of science.
   - Learn how to see; develop your senses.
   - Practice the previous three in the context of the realization that everything connects to everything else.

By learning how your own brain works, you will simultaneously encourage it to perform better. For example, when you realize that one of your brain's prime skills is imagination combined with association, the mere fact of knowing this will automatically set your brain on a path on which it will use these two skills more.

To enhance this process, it is useful, once you have learned about the basic and extraordinarily subtle mechanics of your brain, to learn specific skills, such as Mind Mapping, memory techniques, creative thinking, speed-reading, and a full range of physical skills. The more you learn about your brain and about how to use it well, the more you will create a positive spiral in all areas of your development. *For example, the knowledge that there is no brain cell loss with age in normal, active, and healthy brains can be extraordinarily motivating and encouraging.* We now move on to the most commonly asked question among reader groups and audiences in the 40–50+ age range:

How can I improve my collapsing and failing memory? For instance, you may often have been given a telephone number and forgotten it within two minutes or have been introduced to 10 people and forgotten their names within seconds of being introduced to the tenth. Older people often see this as evidence of their declining mental powers. However, the syndrome is just as common in the young as in the old.

Long-term memory is so automatic that many people don't even realize that it is *memory.* For example, every word of every language you speak daily is a function of your long-term memory. It is also an example of the incredible ongoing power and accuracy of these mental skills.

One often hears people complaining vociferously about their declining mental powers as they age and in particular bemoaning their vanishing powers of memory. Yet they do this with a coherence, eloquence, and masterful recall of language that utterly refutes the point they are trying to make!

Your name, the vast range of your standard knowledge, and your memory of environments and routes are also part of your long-term memory. Both short- and long-term memory can be improved by practicing your powers of concentration, association, and imagination and, as da Vinci suggested, by developing each of your senses. When developed in such a way, each helps the other, and all help you.

> ### Brain Flash
> ### Building a Better Brain
>
> Neuroscientists explore the benefits of brain calisthenics. How you can think faster, improve your memory, and defend against Alzheimer's Disease.
>
> Evidence is accumulating that the brain works a lot like a muscle—the harder you use it, the more it grows. Although scientists had long believed the brain's circuitry was hardwired by adolescence and inflexible in adulthood, its newly discovered ability to change and adapt is apparently with us well into old age. Best of all, this research has opened up an exciting world of possibilities for treating strokes and head injuries—and warding off Alzheimer's Disease.
>
> —*Life* magazine

What Should I Do Now?

1. If you don't already exercise, now is the time to start, now that you know how your brain accepts a Good New Habit.

2. In forthcoming chapters, we give tips on diet. Think about yours: is it unhealthy? Lots of junk food and sugary snacks? If so, now that you know how to ditch the Big Bad Habit, this is the time for change!

3. Similarly, use TEFCAS and your new knowledge of the BBH and GNH to commit to becoming healthier in every way. Your mental powers will improve, and you will live longer to enjoy exercising them.

4. If you wish to develop a particular new mental skill, such as your powers of memory, you now know how to

convince your brain to start the learning process. The metapositive thinking we have described is the way forward.

5. Now that you have established the possibility of developing the brain through stimulation, it is essential to search for a moral or ethical theory that supports the physiological thesis. The next chapter does just this.

CHAPTER 5

The Goethe Gauntlet:

Self-Improvement through Self-Challenge

Wer immer strebend sich bemüht,
Den können wir erlösen.
Striving to achieve is the path to salvation.

Am Anfag war das Wort? Am Anfag war die Tat.
In the beginning was the word? In the beginning was the deed!
—JOHANN WOLFGANG VON GOETHE, *FAUST*

We have now seen that the physiological stimulation of the brain produces dramatic and advantageous changes. The next logical step is to search for an artistic, literary, political, and philosophical basis for the physiological fact—a philosophy of stimulation.

The writings of Goethe, one of the greatest geniuses of all time, provide the philosophical justification for a strategy of self-improvement through self-challenge. we quote (and reinterpret) key lines from Goethe's masterwork *Faust* to do this. The element of self-challenge is crucial, since this is the way to develop the new synaptic connections that physically improve the brain.

The Challenge That Is the Key to This Book

Johann Wolfgang von Goethe (1749–1832) was, and is, for German culture, an amalgam of Shakespeare, Milton, Byron, Dante, Racine, Corneille, and Molière, all rolled into one. Having a gigantic active vocabulary of 50,000 words, he has been regarded as the man with the highest IQ in human history. Goethe was a lawyer, poet, dramatist, novelist, statesman, historian, anatomist, botanist, optician, and philosopher. Pursuing each separate career simultaneously, but with equal commitment and energy, he lived to the healthy age of 83 and died yearning for more, with the words *"Mehr Licht"*—"More light"—on his lips.

Goethe's supreme masterwork was his tragedy *Faust,* written in two parts. This gigantic poem, the greatest dramatic work in German literature, tells the story of Faust, the scientist and philosopher who, in order to pierce the only mysteries still unfathomed by his research, sells his soul to the Devil (Mephistopheles) to gain total knowledge and absolute power. The Faust tragedy is a theme that has powerfully attracted other world-class writers, such as Christopher Marlowe and Thomas Mann, representing, as it does, one of the most poignant myths of Western civilization. But Goethe put a very different slant on it, one that explains his own enormous creative output over such a long life, and one that contains a massively important message for us. Goethe first set out his extensive plan for *Faust*, part 1, in 1797, when he was forty-eight. He spent the remainder of his life working on *Faust*, and it was the final major piece of writing he completed, at the age of eighty-two, in 1831, just nine months before his death.

In *Buzan's Book of Genius*, we presented for the first time the theory of *Goethendipity*, a vital secret known to all possessors of genius. Here we restate this formula in Goethe's own words. Its effectiveness will be immediately apparent to all readers who are determined to improve their own performance, at any age, and in any walk of life.

Over to Goethe:

Act, Do, Be

Until one is committed, there is hesitancy, the chance to draw back, always ineffectiveness. Concerning all acts of initiative (and creation), there is one elementary truth, the ignorance of which kills countless ideas and splendid plans: that the moment one definitely commits oneself, then providence moves too.

All sorts of things occur to help one, that would never otherwise have occurred. A whole stream of events issues from the decision, raising in one's favor all manner of unforeseen incidents and meetings and material assistance, which no man could have dreamed would have come his way.

Whatever you can do, or dream you can, begin it. Boldness has genius, power, and magic in it. Begin it now.

Now, for the first time, we reveal the hidden meaning behind the central passage in *Faust* (quoted below). We call this "the Goethe Gauntlet." It embodies the one central truth for all of you who wish to improve the power and efficiency of your brains as you age.

Make no mistake: this is not a chimera designed to produce an artificial sense of well-being in the gullible. It is a well-attested medical fact, confirmed by the well-known British medical expert Dr. Andrew Strigner, among others: the synaptic connections in your brain grow and improve their powers of association if you present constant fresh challenges to your thinking apparatus.

Constantly seek out fresh stimuli and exciting challenges, and your life will become richer, more interesting, more fun, and ultimately more meaningful.

Relentless Persistence

Once again, over to Goethe. We have reached that scene in *Faust* where the Devil offers Faust every pleasure a human being could possibly desire. Here is Faust's reaction:

Faust: Should I ever lay myself on a bed of ease, then let life be over for me! If you can ever delude me that I have no ambitions left, if you can entice me with a life of pure pleasure, that will be my last day on earth! This is my challenge!

Devil: Agreed!

Faust: Confirmed, not once, but twice! Should I ever say of a particular moment, "Tarry, you are so precious," at that instant clap me in your devil's chains, for I will have lost my great game. The death knell may toll for me then, and you will be free of your service. The clock will stop, the hour hand fall, and, for me, time will be over!*

This message informs every single piece of advice we offer in this book. It is designed specifically for those of you who want to improve your brains as you age and avoid seeing your mental faculties diminish.

Goethe's message, as expressed in those few lines, is one of tireless endeavor, of constant striving. But it must be purposeful and positive effort, pursuing its course in the full consciousness of our place within the grand context of the universe. In this sense, *Faust* is a poem of supreme optimism—it was Goethe's testament to his nation and to the world. As critics have noted, by reason of its sublimely universal content, its breadth of emotional and intellectual appeal, and its wealth and variety of poetic form, *Faust* has earned the right to be placed alongside Virgil's *Aeneid*, Dante's *Divine Comedy*, and Milton's *Paradise Lost*.

Before you embark on the rest of this book—always bearing at the forefront of your mind the Goethean message, through which to view all the forthcoming information, advice, and exercises—it is worth mentioning a possible philosophical counterargument.

Cultivate the Garden

The great French writer and philosopher Voltaire (1694–1778), in his novel *Candide,* famously offered this piece of

---

* (Translation by Ray Keene)

metaphorical advice for those of advancing years: *Il faut cultiver notre jardin* ("We must cultivate our garden").

This, at first sight, anodyne exhortation seems far removed from Goethe's message of constant striving, but look more closely. Voltaire did not write: "We must retire to our garden"; or "We must fall asleep in our garden"; or "We must smoke pot in our garden"; and especially he did not write: "We must drink ourselves senseless in our garden."

Voltaire deliberately, consciously, and subtly used the active word *cultivate*, and in that sense he was at one with Goethe.

What Should I Do Now?

1. Be mentally active. Choose an interesting and challenging goal and pursue it. What are your interests? What are you good at? What do you enjoy doing? Choose a challenge from one of your best fields.

2. Learn dancing; study a new language; play a musical instrument; take up mind sports; start painting. There are dozens of sports to choose from: sailing, mountain biking, martial arts, pickleball—the choices are myriad. Cross Antarctica or climb Mount Everest if you feel really adventurous! The important thing—no matter how great or small the challenge—is to stimulate yourself. If at the same time you can become socially involved with other people and adapt to new situations as they arise, so much the better.

Brain Flash
Stimulation versus Stagnation

To assess the effect of a rich environment on brain growth, psychologist Mark Rosenzweig of the University of California at Berkeley allowed a group of baby rats to grow up in a cage full of ramps, ladders, wheels, tunnels, and other stimuli. A second group was left in barren cages. After 105 days, their brains were examined, showing that the brains of the rats raised in the rich environment were larger than those of the control group. There were also 15 percent more glia cells, and the neuron bodies were 15 percent larger. Perhaps most importantly, there were more interconnections with other neurons.

CHAPTER 6
The First Challenge

*Most noble Emperor, if ever a man could escape
death by learning, then you would be the one.*
—MICHAEL SCOTT, SCHOLAR AND ASTROLOGER
TO THE HOLY ROMAN EMPEROR FREDERICK II

We have seen from chapter 4 that the brain can change physiologically, and from chapter 5 that there is a philosophical justification for pursuing this stratagem. In this chapter we offer a stimulating menu of challenges which are designed to help you take the first steps on the path toward expanding your mental powers, developing the physiological complexity and sophistication of your brain, and accepting the Goethe Gauntlet.

The 10 criteria for the "Brain of the Year" Award are set out below as personal challenges and goals representing your first step on this path. Profiles of some winners of the award are given as inspirational examples.

High Goals and Standards to Set Yourself

Set yourself the ultimate challenge: the goal of being short-listed for, or indeed winning, the Brain Trust Charity's prestigious Brain of the Year Award. Visit WorldMemory Championships.com for details.

The Brain Trust is a British charitable organization dedicated to research and the dissemination of knowledge about cognition, learning, and the brain.

In previous years, this award has been given to Gary Kasparov, the world chess champion; Dr. Marion Tinsley, who defeated the Silicon Graphics Chinook computer at checkers; and celebrity coach and best-selling author Arif Anis. It is presented annually to the individual who best meets the following criteria. Candidates:

1. Must be preeminent in their chosen field of endeavor.
2. Must have contributed major new creative developments to their field of endeavor.
3. Must have made a notable effort to educate other people in their chosen discipline.
4. Must have incorporated the principle of a healthy mind in a healthy body in their lives.
5. Must have exhibited persistence and stamina over time.
6. Must have demonstrated a general cultural awareness.
7. Must have contributed demonstrably to their society.
8. Must have shown a concern for humanity.
9. Must strive to be active and must be known for the enthusiasm of their message.
10. Must be a good role model, both for those in their own field of endeavor and in general.

These ten criteria are superbly challenging goals and standards to set yourself and by which to rate your own performance and improvement.

Previous winners include:

GENE RODDENBERRY

Well into his fifties, Gene Roddenberry, the originator and mastermind behind *Star Trek,* was an engineer, decorated war hero, pilot, social mover and shaker, and visionary. In his early writing career, he was the prime creative force behind the cult television program *Have Gun, Will Travel,* the first Western to feature an intellectual hero, Paladin, whose emblem was the knight chess piece.

Roddenberry, who was a leading member of the American Humanist Association, moved on from there to the creation of *Star Trek,* meeting apparently insuperable barriers to putting on a television series that was initially almost universally ridiculed. The themes that inspired *Star Trek* included racial and sexual equality, the training of the intellect and the body, and the importance of compassion and love.

In Roddenberry's own words: "To be different is not necessarily to be ugly; to have a different idea is not necessarily to be wrong. The worst possible thing that can happen to humanity is for all of them to begin to look and talk and act and think alike. The best measure of maturity and wisdom in a human is the recognition of the value received in hearing another say, 'I disagree with you for the following reasons ...'"

DOMINIC O'BRIEN

Dominic O'Brien, the first World Memory Champion (and eight-time winner), first won the championship in 1991, in the process setting a new world record for the perfect memorization of a 52-deck pack of cards in 2 minutes, 29 seconds. In 1994, he established yet another new world record of 44.78 seconds. (The current world record is 13.96 seconds, set by Zou Lujian of China in 2017.)

O'Brien did not excel in school. As a student, he was diagnosed with dyslexia and attention deficit disorder (ADD) and struggled in both reading and writing. His talent was his ability to visualize, and he believes that anyone, with the proper training, can do what he does. He has dedicated his life to exploring and developing his own memory, creating systems for improving memory, and helping others improve their memorization skills.

DR. MARION TINSLEY

Dr. Marion Tinsley, born on February 3, 1927, was for over 40 years the dominant champion of the world in the game of checkers (known as *draughts* in the U.K.). His greatest achievement was beating the Chinook draughts computer in London in 1992. He died on April 3, 1995.

During Tinsley's span as the dominant checkers player, he engaged in thousands of top-level tournament games and many one-on-one matches at local, national, and world championships. Throughout, Tinsley lost a total of only nine games. Coauthor Ray Keene says, "Apart from Tinsley being the supreme world record-holder in checkers, his accomplishments more than matched the greatest feats of all the giants of the chess world, including Alekhine, Fischer, and Kasparov." Tinsley was undoubtedly the greatest mind sports champion of all time and may justifiably claim to have been the greatest champion of *any* sport.

Brain Flash
The Surprising Vigor of the Oldest Old

The oldest old are healthier than the merely old in several respects. Heart disease and stroke, for instance, have their greatest impact in the fifties through eighties for men, and about 10 years later for women. Those who make it past the danger zones are less apt to be stricken at all. Similarly, Alzheimer's Disease usually picks off its victims by the mid-eighties. Researchers have found that men in their nineties outperformed octogenarians in tests of mental function.

The Grim Reaper himself may slow his pace for the oldest old. While the chance of dying increases exponentially with each year from 50 to 90, the odds rise less steeply after 90.

The vigor of the very old has a simple explanation. The genetically weak die off, and what is left is an enriched group of healthy, strong individuals.

They handle stress incredibly well. A lifestyle of moderation and exercise also helps, as does education. Studies suggest that, on average, better-educated people suffer less mental deterioration in old age.

—*Time* magazine

Asa Long, the former world champion and Tinsley's mentor, estimated that Tinsley had spent 100,000 hours studying checkers. Said Tinsley, "That fact alone should answer a few questions about this 'simple' game."

By 1954 Tinsley was the undisputed world champion, although many checkers historians believe that his real domination started a good seven years earlier. His domination of the game for the following thirty-eight years was so complete that by 1992, at the age of sixty-five, he had completely run out of opposition and decided to retire as undefeated champion. In recognition of his greatness, the checkers world bestowed upon him the title of World Champion Emeritus.

Tinsley's retirement was disturbed by the arrival on the scene of a phenomenally brilliant new player, who cut a devastating swath through the checkers world and became the world's new number one. Intrigued by this new genius, Tinsley accepted a world-title challenge from the prodigy and thus launched a new era in mind sports.

For this new player had a silicon brain. It was a Silicon Graphics computer, code-named Chinook, programmed by Jonathan Schaeffer of the University of Alberta in Canada. The computer could calculate an incredible 3 million moves a minute and had a database of 18 *billion* positions, including all of Tinsley's greatest games. Before the match, most mind sports players and observers exhibited extreme nervousness, afraid that the "Silicon Brain" was going to devastate the human brain and somehow make the latter subservient.

Tinsley, in his typically calm and serene manner, appeared simply amused. When asked by the press whether he was afraid of his prodigious opponent, Tinsley explained that he considered it to be very much like a postgraduate student: "Very bright, very dedicated, willing to work on problems all night while I sleep—but can't really *think*." He went on to explain that he felt supremely confident because, "brilliant though Professor Schaeffer and his team are as programmers, I believe I have a superior programmer—his name is God."

Playing draughts at a level never seen before, Tinsley, at the age of sixty-six, gradually dominated the mechanical mind. He won the 39th game after having played four games a day for as much as twelve hours a day, for two solid weeks—a superhuman feat. This exhibited Tinsley's extraordinary will-power and stamina, as well as his belief that the human brain improves its abilities with age, especially when used well.

On the computer's resignation, Tinsley rose out of his seat, exclaiming, "A victory for human beings."

Perhaps the greatest compliment paid to Dr. Tinsley came from Professor Schaeffer and the Grand Master checkers community. When analyzing the games between Tinsley and the Chinook, they all came to an extraordinary conclusion: if one had not known which was the computer and which the human, the sheer perfection of Tinsley's games would have convinced the knowing observer that the computer's games were those of the human and Tinsley's the product of a perfect intelligence.

As a result of his unprecedented mental accomplishments, Tinsley won the Brain Trust Charity's Brain of the Year Award, which was announced at the Royal Albert Hall Festival of the Mind on April 21, 1995.

ARIF ANIS

In 2021, philanthropist Arif Anis was named Brain of the Year for his outstanding achievements during the coronavirus outbreak, during which he assisted the United Kingdom's National Health Service (NHS) with an ingenious 1 million meals campaign (www.onemillionmeals.uk), which received global recognition.

Anis is also known globally as a thought leader; author of I'MPOSSIBLE, Follow Your Dreams, and The Man in the Arena; and coauthor, with Qaiser Abbas, of Made in Crises. The 2018 edition of the Power100 British Parliamentary Review listed Anis as among the 100 most influential trailblazers in Europe.

Anis has twenty years of experience in delivering trans-formational results, uplifting lives, and impacting people, policies, and narratives. He was awarded the Global Man of the Year Award for 2019 in London by *Global* magazine for his contributions to learning and development.

As an international human capital expert, Anis has trained top coaches, corporate leaders, heads of state, movie stars, and CEOs. As a keynote speaker, he has rubbed shoulders with two US presidents, three British prime ministers, and several other global icons of influence.

Anis supports the British Asian Trust, sponsored by the Prince of Wales (today King Charles III). He is a trustee of the world's largest interest-free microfinance loan provider, Akhuwat, which has disbursed around four million interest-free loans (more than $725 million). His initiatives have been featured by the BBC, ITV, Sky, CNBC, *The Daily Telegraph*, and Yahoo! as well as many other global platforms.

What Should I Do Now?

You may decide to go in for the Brain of the Year Award in a formal way,or not. However, by following the 10 criteria and challenges for candidates, which we have set out in this chapter, you will have created for yourself a clear program, with lucidly stated goals and stages. This will lead to ongoing self-improvement. Try each challenge in turn or simultaneously.

In the next chapter, we face one of the greatest challenges—the all-pervading belief that sexual activity dwindles to zero with advancing age.

CHAPTER 7

Sex and Age

Give me chastity and continency, but not yet.
—St. Augustine

Does sexual activity decline with age—or is it better at seventy? In this chapter, we explore the fallacy that sexual activity is destined by nature to decline over the course of one's life. Sex is both a physical and mental activity, and we show how love acts as a vital brain food. If you stay active, alert, and curious about life, there is no reason why sex through the decades is doomed—in fact, it can be a source of ever-increasing pleasure!

A Seminal and Sexy Story

In a rest home for over-80s in Vancouver, British Columbia, the nurses and staff were having particular difficulty with a ninety-two-year-old inmate. He was a wealthy man, occupying a private suite.

He was the apotheosis of the nightmare resident: truculent, intractable, grumpy, irritable, verbally abusive, permanently dissatisfied, and, when not expressing his anger or dissatisfaction, seriously uncommunicative. His behavior became particularly obnoxious during visiting times, when he was often the only resident without relatives or friends coming to see him.

One day, he asked one of the few nurses with whom he ever communicated if he might arrange for his young niece to visit him. Permission was naturally granted, and on the next visiting day (there were three per week) a vibrant, attractive young woman came to see him. After his niece's visit, the nonagenarian's demeanor perked up considerably, and arrangements were made for his niece to visit him thrice weekly. Her articulate, intelligent, and friendly behavior animated the staff and other patients as well, and her thrice-weekly visits over a period of six months transformed the home.

In particular, the man's behavior became the opposite of what it had been before. Obviously warmed by the affection of a committed family member and stimulated by her lively personality, he became unusually sociable, chatting and bantering with staff and other patients, far more physically and mentally active, and in general a delight to be with.

This happy idyll came to a tragic end when someone inadvertently discovered the "horrible truth": that the gentleman's "niece" was in fact a high-class courtesan, and that rather than simply enjoying stimulating conversations three times a week, the 92-year-old sexual athlete had been having passionate lovemaking sessions instead!

The reactions to these findings were immediate and dramatic. The man was privately and publicly berated for being a dirty old man, his "niece" was banned forever from the home, and he was placed in virtual solitary confinement by everyone in, and connected with, the home.

Predictably, his behavior immediately reverted to its former truculence, and the rest of his short life (arguably far shorter than it should have been) was spent in defiance and misery.

Sexual Perception and Sexual Reality

The above story raises a number of moral issues. It also raises a number of intriguing questions:

1. Why do we see sexual interest and activity as increasingly "dirty" as we get older?
2. Is it natural for men and women to experience strong sexual urges well into their later years?
3. What are the actual patterns of sexual behavior in the human species as it advances through the years?

For your own enlightenment, complete the following quiz. In the table on the next page, rank, in numerical order from 1 to 10, the decade during which you think most sexual activity occurs, the one in which second most activity occurs, third most activity occurs, and so on, until you rank a decade 10, indicating that the least sexual activity occurs then.

Age	Rank
0–10 years	
10–20 years	
20–30 years	
30–40 years	
40–50 years	
50–60 years	
60–70 years	
70–80 years	
80–90 years	
90–100 years	

You might now wish to compare your own thoughts with Tony Buzan's global surveys. These were carried out in over fifty countries throughout Europe, the Middle East, Australasia, and the Americas. The results were surprisingly consistent across language and culture.

These are the general assumptions, although it was often assumed that from sixty—and even fifty onwards—there was no sexual activity or drive at all. What are the facts?

Sexual Facts and Trends

Even with Freud's purported liberation of the libido, the first half of our century was demonstrably *not* liberated in its attitude toward sex and sexual behavior. For example, it was considered a revelation when the initial studies of Masters and Johnson in the 1950s revealed that people over forty actually, and regularly, enjoyed an active sex life.

Age	Rank
0–10 years	5
10–20 years	2
20–30 years	1
30–40 years	3
40–50 years	4
50–60 years	6
60–70 years	7
70–80 years	8
80–90 years	9
90–100 years	10

Table showing global assumptions on the relative amount of sexual activity in the various decades of life.

What numerous studies are now revealing, including the later studies by Masters and Johnson and the Shere Hite Report—to mention but two of the more "blockbuster" studies—is that the reality is very different from the assumption. It increasingly appears that the actual ratings for sexual activity between consenting individuals are probably as shown in the table below.

Age	Rank
0–10 years	10
10–20 years	5
20–30 years	3
30–40 years	4
40–50 years	6
50–60 years	2
60–70 years	1
70–80 years	7
80–90 years	8
90–100 years	9

Table indicating probable actual ranking of relative sexual activity between human beings by decade.

"Impossible!" you might cry, "Sixty to seventy *can't* be number one!" Indeed, when these research findings were first made known at public seminars, the reaction of the audience was not only disbelief but often open derision.

Sexual Activity: The Emerging Picture

But when we investigate everyday life, the popular assumptions become more unreasonable and the new survey findings far more understandable and reasonable.

Let's examine the rankings based on global assumptions in the light of what the evidence shows.

DECADE 0–10

Very little sexuality between individuals. This is obviously because the sexual chemicals have not kicked in, contact is normally limited to public arenas, and societies do not as a rule encourage such behavior.

DECADE 10–20

Far less sexual activity than is often supposed. For many children, the preteen and early teen years continue the habit patterns of their first ten years. Although the *thought* of sexual activity may take up increasing time, the *actual* activity is frequently limited. This is because:

- Much contact is still in public.
- Fear of an unknown area of activity (pregnancy, disease, damage to reputation) inhibits that activity.
- Ignorance of the activity often leads to very brief contact.

- Roiling emotions of the teenage years often lead to hurt feelings and lengthy periods of abstinence.
- Many societies and religions discourage sexual contact between minors.

DECADE 20–30

"Surely this *must* be the most active sexual decade?"

Certainly not "surely."

Consider the statistics and the operational facts of life for those in their twenties. Assuming the average couple is married at the age of nineteen or twenty. Within the first year of marriage, when there is usually considerable sexual activity, they also have to find regular employment, become accustomed to each other's habits, and either rent or purchase accommodation.

Within the second year (they are now twenty-one!), this "average" couple will have their first child. Pressure of work and pressure of paying the bills begin to increase, and by the end of the year the woman is pregnant again. In the following year of their marriage, the second child arrives. If ever there were an energy-draining, contraceptive device, it is two young offspring.

For the rest of the decade, both mother and father are attending to the increasing demands of a growing young family and the accelerating sapping of all their resources, especially finances and time.

Sexual activity is not nearly so active in this period as is generally assumed.

DECADE 30–40

During this decade, work demands, financial worries, and time constraints continue to exert pressure. And the children become *teenagers!* At this stage of their lives, the parents are very like male and female birds in the later stages of spring, who spend their entire day searching for and bringing home food to their screeching fledglings. At the end of the day, there is often hardly enough energy to crawl into bed, let alone make love in it!

Not a particularly active sexual decade.

DECADE 40–50

This decade, as generally predicted by those surveyed, is even less active than the previous one. This is *not* because of any genetic or evolutionary imperative. It is entirely due to lack of opportunity and the fact that enormous energy is being devoted to other areas of activity.

By this decade, the pressures of work are increasingly demanding or crushing. If the individuals progress in their professional careers, they will often be required to work fourteen to sixteen hours a day, six to seven days a week, frequently sacrificing holidays along the way. If the career has for some reason stalled or failed, demotivation, disillusion, and listlessness tend to set in, draining creativity, inspiration, and sexual energy.

Children are often still present, having either moved on to higher education, with all the financial and emotional strains that places upon the parents, or having lingered on in the family home to save themselves the financial burden of finding and paying for accommodation.

DECADE 50–60

The sixties increasingly represent a turning-point in "sexual decline." With a growing number of organizations offering early retirement packages, fifty-five is becoming a not uncommon retirement age. Like a runner gaining energy from seeing the finish line, the person who has worked for thirty years is often reenergized by the thought of their impending freedom.

When retirement at such an age does take place, a whole new world of opportunity arises. The point is poignantly made in the following story.

A couple who had married in their early twenties had worked their hearts and souls out raising a family, both taking on extra work to supplement their standard income. They had raised four children, each born two years apart. The parents had successfully put each child through school, and also through college and university.

The youngest child was about to enter her final year of university; upon graduation, she would immediately go abroad for both travel and work experience. Because of the emotional significance of this last departure from the family nest, the parents drove the girl back hundreds of miles to her university and spent a leisurely few days driving home.

As they entered their driveway, the wife turned to her husband, smiled broadly, and said, "Welcome, my darling, to the honeymoon home."

Your imagination can fill in the sexual details of their lives up to and beyond that magical point in time.

DECADE 60–70

The new number 1!

Why? Because at this time of life, in modern society, tens of millions of individuals are still exceptionally fit, both physically and mentally, wealthy, curious, and ready to enter their second childhood, in the best sense of the word.

A remarkable confirmatory story for this decade of life is that of an Englishwoman whose husband had died in his early sixties.

After mourning for a number of years, she asked her children whether they thought it appropriate if she began to search for a boyfriend. She explained that their father had been the only lover she had ever known and that she seriously wanted to explore sexual life in the way that modern young girls did. Her children agreed that it would be a good idea, though little did they know what amazing stories were to follow.

In the space of three years, this woman was approached by and had love affairs with a fifty-year-old Hungarian, a thirty-three-year-old Italian, a sixty-two-year-old Englishman, a twenty-four-year-old American football player, to mention just a few! When she brought her latest new boyfriend home for acceptance by the family, the usual roles became almost reversed, the children having to admonish the affectionate couple for consistently billing and cooing in public, and for cuddling and fondling each other incessantly.

Opportunities to pursue lifelong dreams are increasingly available, and the chance to explore an intimate relationship with the person with whom you have lived a very public family life is at last possible. In a different scenario, the chance to explore a relationship with a new significant other opens up numerous other avenues for exploration. A delightful story illustrates this point.

At a seminar given by Tony Buzan in the mid-1980s, he was lecturing on the points covered in this survey. At the lunchtime break, a magnificently fit sixty-five-year-old lady rushed up to the stage, grabbed his hand vigorously and, with blazing eyes, said, "Thank you! Thank you! Now I can go home and tell my lover that we are *not* both crazy!"

In addition to all these inviting characteristics and situations is the fact that by this time the individual is far more sexually experienced, considerate, and aware. This means that lovemaking, instead of comprising the rushed physical urgencies of younger generations, can be a more drawn-out, exploratory, experimental, and romantic affair.

DECADE 70–80

In contradiction to the standard stereotype, seventy- to eighty-year-olds are often exceptionally vigorous, energetic, and enthusiastic. As you read this sentence, many septuagenarians will be climbing mountains, running marathons, preparing for the Veterans' Olympics, and making passionate love!

In addition to having amassed a wealth of experience, they have amassed massive capital. Economists estimate that over 70 percent of the world's wealth is owned by those over seventy.

With continued physical and mental vigor, and with vast resources at their disposal, this age group—still bursting with sexual energy—is active.

DECADE 80–90

Little research has been done on this age group. However, initial reports seem to indicate that there is no real change in either sexual desire or activity as people move from their seventies to their eighties.

Mae West, for example, kept a bevy of male lovers to satisfy her undimmed sexual desires throughout her later years. She said they kept her fit, happy, stimulated, and fulfilled, her only complaint being that the younger ones lacked stamina.

This area is ripe for exploration, and the authors commend investigation of this area by the reader!

DECADE 90–100

Stories such as the one that open this chapter abound: of ninety-year-olds who are still exceptionally active in the sexual arena. The great Spanish artist Pablo Picasso was known to prowl the territory around his studios throughout his eighties and nineties in search of young lovers.

It appears that the twin flames of the human spirit and human sexuality burn brightly throughout life, and that the romantic impetus actually increases with age. It is incumbent on each one of us to nurture all three in ourselves and in others.

Derision and Prejudice

When the facts are so apparent, how we can have got it so dreadfully wrong? The answer lies in the fact that most modern nations have brought up children with the erroneous belief that their bodies are somehow dirty, that sex is naughty, and that after the production of children, the function of sexuality is finished.

The sad irony is that children grow up considering their parents to be asexual. They are incapable of imagining that their mother and father ever engaged in the very activity that brought them to life. This belief feeds upon itself, becoming a self-fulfilling prophecy that bridges the generation gap, seeding itself implacably into the future.

Love as Brain Food

Further support for the continued role of sex throughout life comes from brain and nutritional research. It has been found that the brain requires five essential "nutrients" for its survival:

1. Oxygen
2. Food
3. Water
4. Information
5. Love

We all know that the brain must have oxygen, food, and water to function. What is frequently not realized is that information and love are also essential for a healthy and active brain as you age. *Without these essential elements, the brain will degrade and die.*

A simple thought experiment will convince you of the importance of love. Think about the devastating *physical* effects that you would experience (or have experienced) when the person you love convinces you, with a few powerful and well-chosen words, that they not only don't love you but are totally indifferent to your existence. The brain *needs* love and the physical touching and fondling that accompany it.

Brain Flash
Slimline Rabbits

An amusing incident in an experiment on cholesterol intake confirms the brain's need of love. American nutritionist William Glasser was feeding rabbits a diet that was high in cholesterol. The purpose of the experiment was to determine appropriate cholesterol levels and to discover what levels would cause unhealthy increases in weight.

The rabbits in the experiment lived in a number of communal cages. After having been given various differing diets, they were all put on the same high-cholesterol diet. All former variables were kept constant, and it was assumed that all the rabbits would respond in a similar fashion.

Extraordinarily, all but one of the cages of rabbits performed as expected. The exception contained rabbits that were genetically identical to those in the other cages, yet for some inexplicable reason they remained sleek, slim, and healthy while all the rabbits in the other cages gained weight as predicted.

Glasser and his colleagues went into deep analysis, comparing blood samples, checking genetic codes, analyzing the material of the cages, confirming that all environmental variables were indeed identical for all the rabbits, and reviewing their dietary records to look for anomalies.

Every avenue of investigation led to a dead end.

Approximately a week later, with the slimline rabbits maintaining their svelte condition against all predictions while consuming the high-cholesterol diet, one researcher chanced to be passing the research lab late at night when he saw the light on. Going in to investigate, he found one of the night researchers holding one of the renegade rabbits. When asked what she was doing, she explained that the nighttime shift often became very boring. As a passionate lover of animals, and especially of rabbits, she would give herself regular breaks, come into the laboratory, and spend five or ten minutes fondling and playing with the rabbits in this particular cage, to whom she had become attached.

The experiment had provided a stunning result that no one had either planned for or expected. As Dr Glasser put it in his conclusion to the research: "Eat what you like, but get a little loving every day."

Physical Health

Medical science is providing, on a daily basis, evidence that the human body can stay exceptionally fit and strong into its second century, if it is exercised appropriately. The global misconception that after your early twenties, everything sinks into an inevitable and rapid decline is being relegated to the dustbins of history.

A well-exercised body has a pint more blood than a poorly exercised one, with the blood providing a high-octane supply of oxygen to all the organs, especially the brain and the genitals. A stronger heart, beating more slowly and rhythmically, reduces stress and increases confidence. All the organs are able to function more efficiently, the risk of disease is reduced, muscle tone is improved, general alertness and energy levels are raised, and stamina—physical, mental, and sexual—is greatly enhanced.

Throughout life, and especially to guarantee sexual longevity, the following three forms of physical toning should be undertaken approximately three times a week, for at least 20 minutes each:

1. **Aerobics.** Aerobic training is a form of exercise that keeps your heart beating at 110–150 beats per minute. Excellent forms of this kind of exercise include swimming, the use of aerobic machines, cycling, rowing, dancing, running, very rapid walking, and intense lovemaking.

2. **Flexibility.** Babylike gymnastic flexibility can be maintained throughout a lifetime. Former yoga instructor Margery Owens still practices yoga every morning, even though she has had nearly total vision loss due to macular degeneration. And she can still execute a move that many twenty- and thirty-year-olds couldn't possibly do—the splits! Marjorie does not attribute her flexibility to good luck or good fortune, but to discipline—the daily practice of yoga, which she also credits for helping her maintain a sharp mind: "There have been a lot of experts recently saying yoga is good for the memory—and I've been told that I have a very good memory for my age," she said.

3. **Strength.** Muscular strength can similarly be maintained throughout life. Excellent methods for maintaining muscular strength include weight training, rowing, rapid swimming and running, gymnastic dance, isometric training, and the more athletic forms of lovemaking.

Is it worth doing all these? Yes, it is!

A body that radiates health and energy also radiates billions of sexual and other messages to everyone with whom it

---

Brain Flash
Be Flexibly Bodied

Excellent exercises to exercises, aikido, tai chi, swimming, gymnastics, dance, and flexibly minded and flexibly bodied lovemaking.

The *Kama Sutra*, the Indian bible of lovemaking and sexuality, is an excellent handbook.

---

comes into contact. And your body is a far more complex and precious instrument than you may ever have thought. Look at the information below to find out just how incredible the human body is, realize the importance of maintaining fitness, and understand that when you are exploring a loving and sexual relationship, you are exploring a miracle.

The Miracle of the Human Body

If you are going to continue to develop throughout your life, what exactly is it you are going to develop?

Consider these staggering facts about the average human being, which means *you*.

1. Each human is created from a single sperm, one of 400 million produced by the father, and from a single egg produced by the mother. These eggs are so small that it would take 2 million to fill an acorn cup.

2. Within each sperm and egg combination, there is the capacity to create about 300,000,000,000,000 billion humans. Each of them is unique.

3. Each human eye contains 130 million light receptors.

4. Each human ear contains 24,000 fibers, which are able to detect enormous ranges and subtle distinctions in the vibrations of the air.

5. To empower body movement, locomotion, and environmental sensitivity, we have 200 intricately architectured bones, 500 totally coordinated muscles and 7 miles (11 kilometers) of nerve fibers.

6. The human heart beats 36 million times each year, pumping 600,000 gallons (2,727,600 liters) of blood each year through 60,000 miles (96,560 kilometers) of tubing, arteries, veins, and capillaries.

7. If you were to flatten out your lungs, the lung cells would cover an entire tennis court.

8. The blood circulating within the human body contains 22 trillion blood cells. Within each blood cell are millions of molecules, and within each individual molecule is an atom oscillating at more than 10 million times per second.

9. Two million blood cells die each second. These are replaced by 2 million more.

10. The human brain contains approximately 86 billion neurons or nerve cells, which amounts to almost 10 times as many cells as there are people currently inhabiting the planet.

11. The human brain contains 1,000 trillion protein molecules.

12. Each human body has 4 million pain-sensitive structures.

13. Throughout the human body there are 500,000 touch detectors.

14. There are 200,000 temperature detectors in the body.

15. Within each human body, there is enough atomic energy to build any of the world's greatest cities many times over.

16. Since the beginning of time, approximately 110 billion people have inhabited planet earth, each one astoundingly different from all the others.

17. The human olfactory system, or sense of smell, can identify the chemical odorant of an object in one part per trillion of air.

Brain Flash
Sex and the Brain

Throughout your life, your body is a potentially potent sexual force. You may be surprised and pleased to know that it carries a sexual organ that is easily the largest on earth—not your genitals, but your brain! Sex is a physical and mental activity, and the mental side plays the far more powerful part. If you continue to develop your mental intelligence throughout life, especially your imaginative powers, you will be continuing to develop your sexual potency.

The Brain, Sex, Love, and Romance

International journalist Nanci Hellmich surveyed top-selling romance writers to discuss the qualities that were most sexually appealing in heroes and heroines. The results will be particularly satisfying to those who are striving to improve their mental performance as they age.

JUDITH MCNAUGHT (*ALMOST HEAVEN*)

Ideal hero: "Strong, witty, intelligent. All my heroes are good communicators."

Ideal heroine: "Very close to the hero. A sense of humor, intelligent."

HEATHER GRAHAM POZZESSERE (*FORBIDDEN FIRE*)

Ideal hero: "Fun to be with, honest, bright."

Ideal heroine: "Someone who definitely has a mind of her own. Intelligent, smart, willing to take chances."

DONNA HILL (*ROOMS OF THE HEART*)

Ideal hero: "The man of your dreams, strong but can be gentle. Career oriented."

Ideal heroine: "She needs to be strong, determined. Someone who can handle both a career and love life. Intelligent, gentle, usually attractive."

BEATRICE SMALL (*THE SPIT FIRE*)

Ideal hero: "A man who is intelligent, willing to learn from a woman. A man who has a sense of humor."

Ideal heroine: "I like a woman with a sense of humor. You need more than just a beautiful woman who responds to sexual overtures. She needs a brain."

Surprisingly, perhaps, the brain and intelligence came top of the sexual hit parade.

As we showed in the life expectancy chart in chapter 2, if you enjoy regular sex once or twice a week, you can add two years to your standard life expectancy. You can add another two years if your intelligence is above average (the average IQ is 100).

Attitude (Mindset)

We can now see that sex through the decades is not doomed to an inevitable decline. It is a field of endless opportunity, bounteous enjoyment, and infinite possibilities for learning and sharing human intimacies with others.

No matter what your age is, when you carry into the sexual arena a body that is beautifully fit, a mind that is intelligent, creative, agile, and alert, and an attitude that is constantly curious, open, exploratory, childlike, romantic, and concerned, your sex life and partnerships will be ones of growing ecstasy.

What Should I Do Now?

Maintaining your sexual fitness is all about aging agelessly both in mind and body.

1. Exercise at least three days per week. Consider exercising six days a week, alternating days between cardiovascular exercise and strength training.
2. Increase your physical flexibility by stretching daily or practicing yoga, tai chi, or qi gong.
3. Engage your mind with reading, games, puzzles, and educational experiences. Sex is not exclusively physical; in fact, it is mostly in the mind.
4. Make sex a priority in your life, nurture sexual relationships, and explore sexuality with your partner.
5. Find ways to have fun and be romantic with your partner, not just in the bedroom. The more playful you are together outside the bedroom, the more fun you will have inside it.

CHAPTER 8

A Sound Mind
in a Sound Body

Look to your health; and if you have it,
praise God, and value it next to a good conscience;
for health is the second blessing that we mortals
are capable of; a blessing that money cannot buy.
—IZAAK WALTON, *THE COMPLEAT ANGLER*

In chapter 4, we saw that the brain cell is the core of any program for development with age. We now set you yet another challenge—to develop a comprehensive Good New Habit of overall and developing physical health. Only in this way can the billion minibiocomputers that are directing you operate at their maximum capacity and multiply their potentially infinite connections in the most effective manner.

We explain the benefits of exercise and diet in living longer and staying mentally and physically fit, citing expert medical opinion. To achieve a healthy mind, you must constantly strive to house it in a healthy body.

> **Brain Flash**
> **Harvard Study Says:**
> **Strenuous Exercise Will Lead to Longer Life**
>
> Harried executives may shoehorn an occasional squash game or round of golf into their overscheduled lives. Office clerks may sometimes trade a quick bite for a gym class during lunch hours. But if they want to get more out of their exercise routine than a competitive attitude or a leaner look, they are going to have to step up the pace. Researchers tracked 17,300 middle-aged men over 20 years and found that those who exercised vigorously almost every day lived longer than those who broke a sweat only once or twice a week. Half-hearted huffing wasn't enough to make a difference, says Dr. I-Min Lee, who led the study. It does not add years to your life.
>
> —*Journal of the American Medical Association*

Food for Thought—and Exercise Too

What you should eat to maintain a peak of mental and physical stamina and energy is a vital topic. We decided to ask Dr. Andrew Strigner, a British consultant physician with a special interest in nutrition and mental improvement, for his personal advice. This is what he told us, exclusively for this book:

I have always had an interest in nutrition. Sadly, when I began my medical education, I discovered that it was not part of the medical curriculum, the result being that I qualified feeling that I knew little more than my patients. Knowing one's own limitations, however, can stiffen one's resolve. So, continuing the search, I was fortunate to discover the McCarrison Society.

Founded originally by a number of doctors, scientists and veterinary surgeons, it was devoted to the study of the relationship between nutrition and health and to the promulgation of this knowledge.

Subsequently I discovered other researchers worldwide. What I found staggering is the amount of actual knowledge that exists, but which tends to remain with the researchers (some of whom appear not to know of the existence of others in the field) and is only slowly released. Curiously, much of this appears in the popular press, perhaps in magazine articles, and is read by an increasingly interested lay public. They, in turn, are putting pressure on the medical profession, thereby causing the doctors to seek the answers.

Happily, some of our newer medical schools, Oxford and Southampton among others, include nutrition on their curricula.

The study of nutrition is the more fascinating because of the contributions made by people in other disciplines: epidemiologists, anthropologists, paleoanthropologists, anatomists, physiologists, biochemists and, of course, clinicians

Nutrition is especially important for those who plan to have children at a later age.

Health before Conception

Remember that each partner contributes genetic material to the embryo. The health of the father-to-be is as important as that of the mother-to-be. It was, for example, long considered that Down syndrome occurred because the mother was too old to produce a healthy child. Evidence, backed by research reported in France, now indicates that many Down syndrome babies result from a defect in the father, most likely due to faulty nutrition, rather than to age.

Health during Pregnancy

Animal breeders and veterinary scientists have long known that good nutrition of the mature mother during pregnancy is vital, and they have gone to considerable lengths to ensure it. Until recently the same attention has not been paid to human beings. It is now recognized that neural tube defects (lack of proper development of the brain and spinal cord) can be caused by deficiencies in the diet. In the U.K., lack of folic acid, one of the B vitamins, appears often to be the cause, while work in Dublin also implicates a deficiency of vitamin B-12. Other studies indicate that, in some Far Eastern countries, serious zinc deficiencies can produce similar defects.

A Diet for the Brain

For a baby, milk is the most important brain food—human milk. To clarify this, let us give you an example.

At birth, a calf weighs 80–100 pounds (36–45 kilograms). At six months, suckling its mother, it will weigh close to 500 pounds (226 kilograms). In contrast, the human baby, born weighing 7–8 pounds (3–4 kilograms), will weigh only about 14 pounds (6 kilograms) at six months of age.

The difference arises from the fact that cows' milk contains a large amount of protein for body-building, and considerable amounts of saturated fat, which provides the energy for growth. Human milk, on the other hand, contains much less protein, and relatively little saturated fat, but large amounts of unsaturated fatty acids. Some of these, together with other substances called cerebrosides, are designed specifically for the construction of the brain and nerve tissue throughout the body. They are needed because the human brain continues to grow for about three years after birth, whereas the cow's brain hardly alters.

Put briefly, human milk builds big brains, whereas cows' milk makes big bodies.

A Diet for Life

The following recommendations, some of which may run contrary to contemporary opinion, are based on the most recently available dietary knowledge. Full explanations of every statement would require a complete book, so the explanatory notes are necessarily brief. A sound and enjoyable nutritional scheme for a longer and healthier life should include:

Any kind of lean meat, especially wild or game meat (pheasant, partridge, grouse, rabbit, hare, venison), including offals such as liver and kidney. They provide protein, carbohydrate, water, minerals, some vitamins and, importantly, the omega-3 essential fatty acids. These are necessary for the renewal of cell membranes and hormones, for the transport of minerals throughout the body, and for the formation of many of the neurotransmitters, which allow for proper brain and nerve function.

Any kind of fish, including oily fish, such as herring, mackerel, sardine, tuna, and salmon. The latter are also sources of omega-3 essential fatty acids. So much dietary advice is puritanical and off-putting, but think about how much fun you can have with smoked salmon, oysters, lobsters, crabs, and prawns!

A variety of vegetables: leaf, stalk, root, pulse, fungus, mushrooms, broccoli, potatoes, cabbage, spinach, lettuce, peas, beans, onions, garlic, peppers . . . greens in general. These are all important sources of different minerals, vitamins, fiber, and of another group of essential fatty acids, labeled omega-6.

Fruits and berries in moderation and in season. Consume sugary fruits and fruit drinks in small amounts, if at all.

Nuts and seeds. Walnuts, pecans, cashews, almonds, sunflower seeds, and so on are all great sources of protein, fiber, vitamins, minerals, and healthy fats.

Occasional eggs (perhaps 2–3 times weekly). The restriction is not because of the cholesterol content of eggs (which to a healthy person is insignificant) but because too frequent consumption can produce an intolerance in some people. This would be a pity, as eggs are a valuable food for us.

Minimal saturated fat: butter, dairy products, fatty meat from domesticated animals such as lamb, beef, and pork. Nevertheless, these foods cannot be eliminated totally. They carry some fat-soluble vitamins and provides texture and flavor, but their main value is as a concentrated source of energy. Anyone undertaking considerable physical effort or living in very low temperatures would require this fuel to meet their energy expenditure.

Eliminating sugar and processed foods, such as cookies and cakes. Although the body uses sugar (glucose) as its main fuel, it prefers to produce its own from the food that we eat and to maintain the correct levels. Too much sugar in the diet upsets this mechanism. Sugar is also one factor significantly linked to heart disease.

Grains (cereals, especially wheat-based products) should be used with moderation and great care. Rye bread can often be tolerated more readily than wheat.

Milk and milk products should similarly be used with caution.

In evolutionary terms, the last three items are relatively new to our diet. There is firm evidence to show that a significant proportion of people can develop an intolerance to milk and wheat proteins.

We are told that milk is needed for calcium: not true! Think fit. No animal takes milk after it leaves its mother, yet each develops bones and teeth. There is, in fact, calcium in almost all the foods that we eat, and more than an adequate amount would be provided in the program that we have outlined for you.

To emphasize the undoubted and powerful connection between proper nutrition and mental ability, we quote a letter from John Harris, a reader of Ray Keene's *Times* chess column:

> I was never very good at chess, but I played a lot and improved tremendously in a prison camp in the war in Kuching, Sarawak. We had an old chap called Poole, who was Blue Funnel's marine superintendent in Batavia, and he was good: he had played as one of 40 simultaneous players against one of the greats, world champion Alekhine, and was the only one to win his game. He taught me several basic principles to follow.
>
> It was at chess that I first noticed the signs of mental deterioration that resulted from our desperate shortage of food. Around the middle of 1944, I found I could no longer visualize moves as far ahead as I had once been able to, and this became progressive.
>
> Fortunately, nearly all, if not quite all, of one's mental faculties recovered, provided that the body did.

An optimistic note of phoenixlike mental resurrection.

Aerobic Exercise

Aerobic exercise increases the efficiency with which air is taken in and oxygen is transported around the body. All aerobics involve deep breathing and repetitive pumping movements of the arms and legs. For maximum benefit, aerobic

Brain Flash
Good Health Is Working Out

It looks like any other council-run leisure center, but The Lagoon in Hailsham, West Sussex, seems more of a shrine. Government Ministers, doctors, and academics from all over Britain have been there and marveled at its curative powers.

Many years ago, GP David Hanraty began prescribing exercise sessions for his sickest patients at the center. The results astonished him. An overweight, sixty-seven-year-old, hypertensive diabetic was able to come off the drugs he had been prescribed; after six months of exercise, he had no symptoms of diabetes at all. Not all the results were so dramatic, but all the participating patients felt significantly better—whether they had depression, coronary disease, or cancer of the rectum.

Since then, 70 local GPs have started to prescribe exercise at The Lagoon and 3,000 patients have benefited.

A serious accident had left George Crew partially paralyzed. His wife Phyliss had a bent back. The couple, who were in their seventies at the time, both reported feeling better and being able to move about more easily since they started swimming at the Hailsham center.

Prescribed exercise has also worked wonders for people trying to stop smoking, for post-natal depression, and for chronic mental conditions. "I sent a patient of mine with schizophrenia down to the center," says Dr Hanraty. "Now she's on much less medication and better able to manage her condition." How does it work? Dr Hanraty believes that exercise boosts self-esteem and stimulates the immune system.

—*The Observer*

exercise should be undertaken for at least 20 minutes three times a week. As with all exercise, however, this applies only to those in good physical condition. If you are in the slightest doubt or have any history of heart trouble, consult your doctor or physician first.

There are many types of aerobic exercise, including brisk walking, jogging, cycling, rowing, dancing, skipping, swimming, squash, tennis, skating, cross-country skiing, slow long-distance running, and circuit training with weights. Some of these (dancing, walking, jogging, swimming) also have a social element. If the very idea of exercise is anathema to you, what about a brisk walk with your favorite dog?

There are numerous ways to exercise at home or in the gym. Among the many exercise machines available, one good possibility is an indoor rowing machine. Rowing provides a total body workout, exercising the heart, lungs, and circulatory system while shaping and toning the muscles of your legs, back, shoulders, and stomach. The wide range of motion involved also improves and maintains your flexibility. Because rowing is an impact-free exercise, the joints are protected too.

The key to sustaining an effective exercise program is feedback. A variety of fitness monitoring devices are now available—either built into exercise machines or wearable. These devices can monitor your pace, calorie expenditure, distance, target output level, time, and heart rate. Many performance monitors also include a memory function, which you can use to review your workout after you have finished.

Brain Flash
Drink and Raise Your IQ

Recent good news comes from Age and Aging, *which reports that the work of Dr Stephen Iliffe, of the Whittington Hospital, suggests that elderly male drinkers score better in intelligence tests than non-drinkers. The study also showed that more than 96 percent of those observed kept within the strict drinking limits recommended by the British Medical Association, and that the rise in intelligence was thus related to moderate, "intelligent," intelligence-raising intake.*

—The European magazine

This finding is entirely consistent with our conclusions about drinking intelligently, as seen in the life expectancy chart in chapter 2. According to this, both heavy drinkers and nondrinkers score less well in terms of life expectancy than moderate drinkers.

Remember: if you are trying to change and improve your diet, and/or trying to take up aerobic exercise for the first time, our advice in chapter 4 on transforming a Big Bad Habit into a Good New Habit will be of paramount importance to you.

Now look at the table on the next page, which advocates sensible drinking as an antidote to heart disease, one of the industrialized world's most prolific and widespread killers. This chart shows that, throughout Europe, the number of deaths from heart disease per 100,000 people declines in relative proportion to the amount of wine drunk per capita per year, up to a maximum of 15½ gallons (70 liters) of wine per annum.

How Wine Consumption Reduces Heart Disease

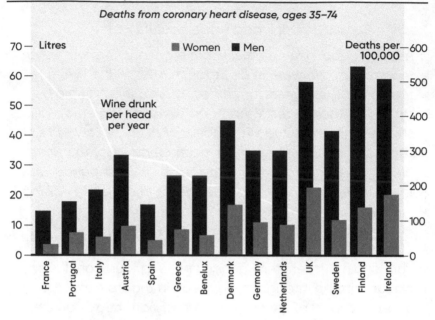

Deaths from coronary heart disease, ages 35–74

Alternating Cardio Workouts with Strength Training

Most athletic trainers and many doctors recommend alternating cardiovascular workouts, such as jogging and cycling, with strength training, such as weightlifting. The reason is that cardiovascular workouts are catabolic, while strength training is anabolic. *Catabolic* refers to chemical reactions that break down large molecules into smaller ones, such as breaking down proteins, fats, or carbohydrates to extract energy. *Anabolic* refers to chemical reactions that build large molecules, such as proteins, from smaller molecules, such as amino acids.

All cells that make up your body need energy to maintain health and function. Your body will get the energy it needs from the foods you eat or from breaking down stored carbohydrates, fats, and (if neither of those is readily available) proteins (such as muscle). If you do too much cardio (catabolic) without strength training (anabolic), you run the risk of depleting your body's stored energy reserves to the point at which your body becomes more susceptible to illness.

In addition, strength training, when done properly, builds muscle by creating microscopic rips in the muscle fibers which heal over the course of about twenty-four hours. By alternating strength training with cardio workouts, you give your muscles the 24 hours they need to heal.

One approach to alternating cardio workouts with strength training (an approach that's gaining popularity), is high-intensity interval training (HIIT). With HIIT workouts, you typically wear a heart monitor and alternate periods of high-intensity exercise with light exercise or rest; for example, 30 seconds of jumping rope at your target heart rate followed by 60 seconds of planks, lifting weights, or walking at a comfortable pace.

Raise Your Intelligence, Lower Your Blood Pressure: Get a Pet

Warwick Anderson, of the Baker Medical Research Institute in Melbourne, has produced the best evidence so far that pets support our mental (and physical) health. Anderson examined 5,741 people aged between twenty and sixty—784 of whom were pet owners—by offering them free health-risk evaluations.

Pet owners turned out to be less stressed mentally and to have significantly lower levels of cholesterol, as well as lower blood pressure. The results were similar across groups who dieted differently, or who were in different socioeconomic categories.

James Serpell, who founded the Companion Animal Research Group at the University of Cambridge in 1985, believes that the difference between the two groups is impressive and that it is "stronger than improvements found in comparable studies on people who have switched to vegetarian diets or taken up exercise programs."

Pet Power

This new research ties in with our life expectancy chart in chapter 2, which suggests that having close friends increases your longevity. The companionship offered by a beloved pet may tie in with this. Stroking a pet is known to decrease stress and high blood pressure and to produce a general feeling of well-being—so much so that in some homes for the elderly, it has been discovered that residents relax and cut down their intake of sleeping pills if a cat is present to be caressed and stroked. Do you want to get fit, stay healthy, reduce stress levels, and live a long life? Getting a pet could be the answer.

Da Vinci's Sleep Formula

Legend tells us that Leonardo da Vinci catnapped for fifteen minutes every four hours, giving him, for example, a total of an hour's extra sleep during a sixteen-hour work day.

According to Claudio Stampi, a researcher at the Institute of Circadian Physiology in Boston, this unorthodox sleep schedule makes biological sense. Most animals, he says, naturally sleep this way.

During a three-week study, a graphic artist who adopted da Vinci's format enjoyed it so much that he volunteered for follow-up experiments. Additional studies of solo ocean racers suggest that the contestants with the shortest sleep episodes do better than those who sleep for longer periods.

Where possible, and where appropriate, Stampi advocates gentle experimentation with da Vinci's approach to sleeping.

It should be recalled that, in the life expectancy chart, two years should be deducted from standard life expectancy if you sleep for more than ten hours consecutively on a regular basis.

What Should I Do Now?

1. Improve your diet. Eat a regular, substantial breakfast. Avoid binge drinking (consuming excessive amounts of alcohol in a short period of time).

2. Drink sufficient fluids. Herbal teas are highly recommended. Coffee and nonherbal tea are fine, but avoid sweet drinks and be cautious if you feel you "can't get by without them."

    Thirst and sweat should tell you how much to drink; drink when you're thirsty, and drink more when you sweat more. Use the color of your urine as a guide. Your urine should be light yellow. If it's clear, you're probably drinking more than you need. If it's dark yellow or orange, you probably need to drink more.

3. Cows' milk, grains, wheat-based products such as pasta and bread, processed foods, and fruits that are out of season are (evolutionarily) new additions to our regular diet. They can, therefore, often cause allergies, sensitivities, or intolerances. That is why you should be careful about consuming them.

4. Exercise regularly—at least three times a week for at least 30 minutes per session.

5. Take medical advice before embarking on a strenuous program or if you want to exercise but suspect that you suffer from a physical weakness in any area.

6. Consider the following: brisk walking in a park, on a common or in the countryside (with a dog—if you have one that doesn't slow you down or stop every 10 seconds to smell something nasty); jogging; long-distance running; training for marathons; cross-country skiing; rowing; cycling; dancing; swimming; and skating.

7. Join a tennis, swimming, martial arts, or skating club, or a gym, to increase your circle of friends and your general social awareness.

8. Remember that "petting" is good for people and pets.

9. Take catnaps.

10. Be sensitive to the connection between what you eat, when you eat, how much you eat, and how your mind and body perform, and adjust accordingly to optimize how fit you feel mentally and physically.

Your physiological and psychological "ducts" are now all in alignment. Your body should be becoming healthier, so you are ready to work specifically on developing your clarity and fluency of thought as you grow older, within the context of physiological and psychological health. In order to do this, it is essential that you find the right formulas for turning on the gigantic generators of your mind. In the next chapter we reveal a secret weapon that will allow you to do this—a tool that has become known as the Swiss Army knife of the brain.

CHAPTER 9
Mind Maps:
The Secret Weapon

This chapter concentrates on the improved organization of your thoughts and mental processes that can be brought about by using Tony Buzan's invention, the Mind Map. It specifically addresses the problems outlined in chapter 3: the top 20 areas of mental performance requiring improvement among 40- to 50-year-olds.

Adopting Mind Mapping techniques in your business, in everyday life, in presentations, even in making personal to-do lists, can combat the disorganized thinking that is often mistaken for the symptoms of encroaching old age and mental decline.

Mind Mapping

Ray Keene has this to say about Mind Mapping: if you work in a business, academic, service, or industrial environment, you will find Mind Mapping invaluable. When I was invited to lecture at the Royal Institution, London, on whether chess computers will ever defeat human world champions, I made the presentation, which had to last 60 minutes precisely—no

---

Brain Flash
Diagrams Transform the World of Algebra

Simple pictures, rather than reams of bewildering calculations, could be the key to improving mathematics and physics teaching.

A study of great scientists, such as Sir Isaac Newton, has found that they used myriad sketches to uncover the laws of physics. Today's students have to plough through masses of algebraic problems. Many are left with scant understanding of the underlying reality, and it is thought that unenthusiastic and mediocre graduates in such fields as astronomy and engineering are the result.

Researchers have harnessed the picture-book approach of scientific geniuses into a computer system which might inspire students to greater things. It reveals to them the Laws of Motion and of the Conservation of Momentum and Energy, using moving diagrams.

Dr Peter Cheng, a psychologist at the Economic and Social Research Council's Center for Development, Instruction and Training in Nottingham said: "The system allows you to draw diagrams using geometric shapes to find the answers to problems. They make the algebra come alive."

—The Times

---

more and no less. I used a Mind Map. It worked to the nanosecond, and afterwards I was most gratified when the academics and professors of the institute crowded around the podium to wonder at this new form of lecture notes.

Tony Buzan now recounts the genesis of his revolutionary Mind Mapping concept.

The Genesis of Mind Mapping

The first major step occurred when I was 14. I was given numerous tests on intelligence, reading speed, and memory and was told that I would never be able to change the results. As well as infuriating me, this was difficult to understand. After all, physical exercise makes you stronger, so why should mental exercise not improve your mental performance?

I immediately began to work on this problem and realized that if I had the right technique, my results would surely improve. At this stage, I also realized that the least productive method of understanding a subject was to take the kind of notes my teachers and lecturers commonly expected. I found them boring and worthless, and the more notes I took, the less I seemed to understand the material.

At the age of twenty, while I was studying at the University of British Columbia, I began to work seriously on improving my memory and note-taking. This work developed into two branches.

1. I studied the nature of memory. This inevitably includes imagery and association.
2. I studied the note taking methods of the great brains. I observed that, without exception, they all used images, pictures, arrows, and other connective devices, while those who did less well in academic studies made only lincar notes.

The result of this study was Mind Mapping. The more I discovered, the more excited I became. I felt like the discoverers of Tutankhamun's tomb. First of all, I peered through a keyhole and saw the vague shapes of what might be fantastic artifacts. Then I entered the barely lit room and witnessed the incredible potential of its contents. Finally, I managed to cast light on the wealth of treasure I had discovered.

I wanted very much to tell the world about my discovery, and I still do. The first communication of it came with publication of my *Use Your Head* book and the BBC television series of the same name, which was repeated every year for ten years. Major dissemination of the idea involved 15 years of worldwide traveling on lecture tours to academic, business, and government institutions. Then came the establishment by Vanda North of the Buzan Centers, where Radiant Thinking instructors are trained in these educational methods.

The Mind Map is a powerful graphic technique, which provides a universal key to unlocking the potential of the brain. It harnesses the full range of cortical skills—word, image, number, logic, rhythm, color, and spatial awareness—in a single, uniquely powerful manner. In so doing, it gives you the freedom to roam the infinite expanses of your brain. The Mind Map can be applied to every aspect of life where improved learning and clearer thinking will enhance your performance. Mind Maps are now used by millions of people around the world, from the ages of 5 to 105, whenever they wish to use their brains more efficiently.

Like a road map, a Mind Map will:

1. Give you an overview of a large subject area.
2. Enable you to plan routes and make choices.
3. Let you know where you are going and where you have been.

4. Gather and hold large amounts of data.
5. Encourage both daydreaming and problem-solving by revealing creative pathways.
6. Be extremely efficient.
7. Be enjoyable to look at, read, muse over, and remember.

Mind Map Laws

Before you start creating your own Mind Maps, familiarize yourself with the basic principles:

1. In the center of a blank, unlined page of paper, draw an image of the desired topic, using at least three colors.
2. Use images, symbols, codes, and dimension throughout your Mind Map.
3. Select key words and print, using capitals or lowercase letters.
4. Each word or image must be alone and on its own line.
5. The lines must be connected, starting from the central image. In the center, the lines are thicker, organic, and flowing, becoming thinner as they radiate outwards.
6. Make the lines the same length as the word or image.
7. Use colors—your own code—throughout the Mind Map.
8. Develop your own personal style of Mind Mapping.
9. Use emphasis and show associations between different related topics in your Mind Map.
10. Keep the Mind Map clear by using numerical order or outlines to surround your branches.

Keep in mind that Mind Maps are personal. Their purpose is to increase *your* understanding, retention, and creativity. As you create your own Mind Maps, you will discover techniques and styles that work better for you than they might work for me or anyone else. Use what works best for *you*.

How to Mind-Map

Here is the step-by-step process for creating a Mind Map:

1. Place a large white sheet of paper horizontally, or use a Mind Map pad.
2. Gather a selection of colored pens, ranging from thin tip to highlighter.
3. Select the topic, problem, or subject to be Mind-Mapped. This will be the basis of your central image.
4. Gather any materials, research, or additional information that is needed, so that you have all the facts at your fingertips. Now start to draw your central image in the center of your page.
5. Start with an image approximately 2½ inches high and wide for A4 (roughly equivalent to 8½ x 11) paper, and 4 inches for A3 (11 x 17 inches).
6. Use dimension, expression, and at least three colors in the central image in order to attract attention and aid memory.
7. Make the branches closest to the center thick, attached to the image and "wavy" (organic). Place the Basic Ordering Ideas (BOIs) or chapter headings on those branches.
8. Branch thinner lines off the end of each appropriate BOI to hold supporting data.
9. Use images wherever possible.

10. The image or word should always sit on a line of the same length.

11. Use colors as your own special code to show people, topics, themes, and dates and to make the Mind Map more attractive.

12. Capture all your ideas (or those that others have contributed), then edit, reorganize, beautify, elaborate, or clarify them as a second and more advanced stage of thinking.

What Should I Do Now?

Look at the uses and benefits of Mind Maps, which are clearly set out for you in the table below.

THE USES OF MIND MAPS

Uses	Benefits
1. Learning	Reduce workload; feel good about study, review, and exams. Have confidence in your learning abilities.
2. Overviewing	See the whole picture, the global overview, at once. Understand the links and connections.
3. Concentrating	Focus on the task for better results.
4. Memorizing	Easy recall. See the information in your mind's eye.
5. Organizing	Parties, holidays, projects, etc. Make the project make sense to you.
6. Presenting	Speeches become clear, relaxed, and alive. You can be at your best.
7. Communicating	Communicate in all forms with clarity and conciseness.
8. Planning	Orchestrate all aspects, from beginning to end, on one piece of paper.
9. Meetings	From planning to agenda, chairing, taking the minutes, these jobs can be completed with speed and efficiency.
10. Training	From preparation to presentation, make the job easier.

Uses	Benefits
11. Thinking	The Mind Map will become a concrete record of your thoughts at any stage of the process.
12. Negotiating	All the issues, your position, and maneuverability on one sheet.
13. Brainblooming	The new version of brainstorming, generating more thoughts and assessing them more appropriately. Some believe that the more ideas generated, the more the quality declines. In fact, the reverse is true. The more you generate ideas and the greater the quantity, the more the quality increases. This is a key lesson in understanding the nature of your own creativity.
14. Lectures	When you attend a lecture, use a Mind Map to keep a vivid visual memento of it.

If you look closely at these uses of Mind Maps, you will see that they clearly, cogently, and powerfully address certain problems of mental performance. Indeed, they address the top twenty concerns about mental performance expressed by the forty to fifty-plus age group of executives and business leaders.

CHAPTER 10

The Einstein Equation:

A New Challenge

$$E = mc^2$$

—ALBERT EINSTEIN

Now that you have learned how to use the ultimate mental tool, let's turn to examples of some of the great geniuses who expressed their genius between the ages of forty and ninety.

Later in this chapter we provide a self-challenging chart of the qualities you need to develop in order to manifest your own burgeoning intelligence.

The Genius Quest

The ultimate mental accolade is to be regarded as a genius. We now comment on some of the key qualities that have led to such recognition. Can you train yourself to emulate these qualities, Goethe-style?

Our definition of genius encompasses many features that the great minds have in abundance. Among them are mental

---

Brain Flash
The Nature of Genius

Some commonly held theories about genius and creativity—
that people are born geniuses, or that it is a gift from God—
are myths.

   Shortly before his death, Albert Einstein admitted,
"I know quite certainly that I myself have no special talent. Curiosity, obsession, and dogged endurance, combined with self-criticism, have brought me my ideas." And
the inventor Thomas Edison echoes this notion: "Godlike
genius—godlike nothing! Sticking to it is the genius."

---

and physical strength. Even those geniuses who are physically
handicapped find the strength to fulfill their vision and goals.
Cambridge physicist Stephen Hawking, for example, wasn't
expected to live long past fifty. Instead, he lived to the age of
seventy-six and continued to be productive in his later years,
emulating Newton and Einstein in the depth of his revelations about science.

   The definition of *genius* goes on to include recognition of
truth. After all, many people waste energy pursuing false theories or ideas. Genius also involves a love of the task; faith,
vision, passion, commitment, planning; the ability to bounce
back from mistakes; knowledge of the subject; a positive mental attitude; imagination; courage; and energy. Compare these
with the qualities of the brain champions given in chapter 6.

   One of the most extraordinary examples of mental achieve-
ment that we ever witnessed came when we saw Dominic
O'Brien in action at the 1993 Memoriad—a mental Olympics.
Among numerous other feats, he recalled 100 spoken digits

(read out at a rate of one every two seconds) perfectly on two occasions. When we first witnessed this, we were shocked. We had never seen anything like it and found it difficult to accept that this was possible. We had seen brilliant chess players, such as Garry Kasparov, producing phenomenal combinations, but what Dominic O'Brien achieved equaled any of these. In the first Memoriad in 1991, he had achieved some impressive results, but now he was suddenly remembering something like 1,000 written digits, when previously it had been 200, or 15 packs of cards in one hour instead of two. When we first saw it done, we found it totally awesome, and still do.

Historically speaking, many achievements by many different people have struck us. Here are just a few examples:

Gerontological Marvel

We were deeply impressed by Michelangelo's achievement in beginning construction on the Dome of St Peter's in Rome at the age of sixty-three, a task that he continued with utter dedication until the age of eighty-nine. The pope commissioned him to undertake the task. Rather than whining about being too old or too tired, Michelangelo simply got on with it and produced one of the most brilliant works of art and architecture in history.

To the Ends of the Earth

A fact that is not often appreciated about the explorer Christopher Columbus is that he was the first modern European voyager to risk striking directly away from the coastline. Previous explorers were terrified that they might lose their way back or fall off the edge of the earth. No one had ever directly crossed the Atlantic Ocean from Europe to locate a new continent previously unknown to them. The only possible precedent was set by Polynesian seafarers, who did branch out but tended to hop from island to island, rather than sail out into the ocean at right angles to the coast. Columbus's great navigational insight was that the trade winds worked in both directions, so he was confident that he had a means to return to his base. Columbus was 41 years old when he set off on the world's first transatlantic voyage.

Blind Žižka

Johan (or Jan) Žižka, a particular hero of Ray Keene's, was a Bohemian general from the fifteenth century who fought at the famous battle of Agincourt, in 1415, between the English and French armies.

He lost an eye in a later battle, thus rendering him completely blind, as he had already lost the other one in an earlier campaign. Nevertheless, at the age of fifty-one, he went on to win twelve major battles against the Holy Roman Empire, usually against extraordinary odds. His forces (which often consisted of untrained peasants) would typically be outnumbered about 10 to 1 by the opposing army and yet emerged victorious time after time. He had immense energy and was stopped in his tracks only when he caught the plague and died. When we realize that, even by 1900, the average life expectancy in Europe was only fifty, his was quite an achievement.

> ### Brain Flash
> ### Synapse Increasers
>
> Both Albert Einstein and Winston Churchill probably increased their synapses like crazy by practicing art forms that seemed to have little to do with their everyday lives. Einstein played the violin, while Churchill painted land-scapes.
>
> —*Life* magazine

Keeping a Military Machine Uncertain

Werner Heisenberg was a physicist who discovered the uncertainty principle. Loosely speaking, this states that you can never quite pin down atomic particles, because as your knowledge of their position improves, there is a corresponding decrease in your knowledge of their momentum. He realized that this was not just some weakness in the experimental apparatus or the mathematics, but a fundamental law of nature.

This was brilliant enough in itself, but Heisenberg also played a crucial role in the development of atomic weapons during the Second World War. He was, at the age of forty, Germany's leading expert on nuclear physics, but his work had been dismissed by the regime. When they realized, that he probably would be able to help them build an atomic bomb, the authorities changed their tune. Although aware that the project was perfectly feasible, Heisenberg managed to persuade them that it could not work, citing all sorts of technical and practical difficulties. His elaborate deception continued for about four years. Had it not worked, the outcome of the Second World War might have been very different.

There is no single (or simple) intellectual telltale sign of genius, such as linguistic or mathematical ability, but the above examples all demonstrate an amazing persistence in an effort to achieve their vision. These individuals were all highly focused on their goals, subordinating all other factors to them. Motivation is a key factor in the definition of genius.

Another recurrent trend is that geniuses treat the whole planet as one gigantic IQ test and relish accepting the challenges thrown at them.

How to Make the Most of Your Mental Abilities

Decide what you want to do and how important it is to you. Then determine if you are sufficiently motivated to carry it through to its conclusion. *You cannot get this knowledge from others—you must decide for yourself.*

Often we are not sure what is really important to us, so we think making a list is a good idea. An even better idea, as you will probably have realized by now, is to make a color Mind Map of your priorities. Map out all the things that interest you and then rate them in terms of how important they are to you.

You may, for instance, decide that you want to increase your income and concentrate on finding a new job, or on becoming better rewarded for the one you do. Alternatively, you may decide that the most important thing for you is to enjoy your holidays more, so you may learn a new language or explore a foreign culture, which would have the by-product of being mentally stimulating. The possibilities are endless and will, of course, differ from person to person, but *the key factor is motivation.* If you are motivated enough to do what you want to do, everything else will fall into place. People who are not motivated are unfocused and unable to concentrate their energies effectively.

What the Geniuses Teach Us

Successful achievement does not materialize out of nothing—it requires planning, plus a tremendous amount of hard work. Admiration for your peers and a desire to emulate them is another important factor. Many artistic careers are fashioned along the following logical lines: "I want to become a great artist. X and Y are great artists whose work I admire. I will, therefore, study the lives of X and Y and try to emulate them." Machiavelli talks about the importance of emulation in his book *The Prince.* If you are inspired, you copy and then surpass your role models. If you aren't inspired, you can't achieve anything. Cynicism is the enemy of genius.

The Self-Challenging Chart

Here is our selection of mental and physical challenges to enhance your life as you mature:

1. Mind Mapping
2. Learning and study (e.g., history, philosophy)
3. Memorizing
4. Speed-reading
5. Creative thinking
6. Intelligence: IQ

7. Mathematics, science, astronomy
8. The arts (e.g., music, dance, painting)
9. Physical skills and sports
10. Vocabulary and language
11. Presenting and communicating
12. Personality development
13. Games and mind sports (e.g., chess, checkers, bridge, go, Scrabble)
14. Martial arts (aikido, judo, or karate)
15. Travel (exploring, mountaineering)

Once you have examined these, you can then prioritize items by highlighting the new skills that particularly interest you, listing them in the order you decide to work on them:

1. _____
2. _____
3. _____
4. _____
5. _____

Even better, map them out on a Mind Map.

Then monitor your changes and improvements over the years. Observe yourself getting better! To assist you, many activities have official assessment levels or certifications by which you can objectively gauge your own performance. Chess federations, for example, regularly publish sanctioned ranking lists; organized martial arts clubs have their "belt" and "dan" systems; while the authors of this book have instituted a title and rating system for memory performance.

Write to or join the International Brain Club (Tony Buzan International Ltd., info@tonybuzan.com), if you want to know, for instance, how to contact a Mind Mapping, memorizing, mind sports, or martial arts group, society, or association (www.TonyBuzan.com).

Expanding Frontiers

As our knowledge expands and we come to know more about the planet and the universe, our opportunities also expand. We now know that human potential is virtually limitless and that as knowledge increases, so does our capacity to absorb it. So, apart from the possibilities of shining in a particular field, we can also enjoy the attraction of becoming polymaths, people of great or varied learning, like Leonardo, Michelangelo, and Goethe.

The capacity to turn negatives into positives is another excellent indicator of genius. This is not merely a case of fighting through adversity but implies a conscious decision to look for the positives in what appear to be the most appalling circumstances.

Jose Luis Borges, the Argentinean writer had gone blind by his mid-50s but he then learned Old English, which greatly enriched his life. And we have already observed the inspirational examples of Hawking and Žižka.

This is a recurring theme. Many of the geniuses of history are great survivors, who have suffered the most dreadful calamities but have refused to look at them negatively.

On a lighter note, we are great fans of the *Star Trek* series. In many episodes, the *Enterprise* and its crew find themselves in some appalling situation, and the only solution is to think their way out of trouble. As Spock said in one episode, during which he was fatally irradiated, "There are always possibilities."

What Should I Do Now?

1. Pick a genius (or geniuses) of particular interest to you. It could be Leonardo da Vinci, for his versatility; Beethoven, for his determination and heroism in the face of encroaching deafness; Columbus, for his courage and conviction.
2. Mind-Map the qualities of your chosen genius(es).
3. Apply the lessons to your own life.
4. Pick one or more skills from the table presented earlier in this chapter and pledge yourself to become an expert in that area or areas. Start by Mind Mapping your chosen approach.

CHAPTER 11

Achieving
Memory Mastery

*The mastery of some simple mnemonic system may
lead some people to realize, for the first time, that they
can control and modify their own mental processes.*

—HANS EYSENCK, EXPERT ON IQ

In this chapter we address one of the most pervasive and destructive delusions that the human race has so far devised: that as the human brain gets older, it degenerates, losing brain cells and experiencing rapid decline in memory, creativity, mathematics, and linguistics.

In previous chapters, we provided increasing evidence that this is not the case. Now we bang the last nail into the coffin of a ludicrously fallacious idea. Failing memory is, perhaps, the chief mental problem lamented by *everyone*. But memory loss as we get older is not inevitable or necessary.

We now show you how to acquire and learn simple memory techniques (nothing too technical) and give further inspirational examples, this time of memory performance.

Exploring the Amazing Memory Machine

We define *memory* not as a passive recorder of everyday data, pleasant or unpleasant, but as an active, focused laser beam of the mind that you can use to stay ahead mentally. If you train your memory (and we have already observed the dynamic influence that Mind Mapping can exert in this respect), the data will be at your fingertips to conquer new areas of subject knowledge, to run your organization more efficiently, to make more effective presentations—in short, to be increasingly decisive and creative. This chapter recounts key historical moments in the development of memory techniques and portrays some awe-inspiring memory feats to stimulate your own achievements.

First, we examine the hard scientific evidence, showing that memory powers do not alter significantly at any age as long as you continue to use your abilities and do not let them atrophy.

Scientific Evidence on Memory Loss with Age— or Otherwise

Memory loss associated with age may be more a reflection of how we view older people, how they view themselves, and how we test them in the laboratory than of actual memory decline due solely to the aging process. While test results do often reveal poor memory performance in the elderly, two factors that have been shown to confound these results are level of interest and the use of timed performance.

Richard Restak, in his book *The Mind*, spent a great part of his chapter on aging stressing that we do see a decrease in

> **Brain Flash**
> **Old Dogs**
>
> Old dogs rarely have real difficulty learning new tricks; they more often have difficulty convincing themselves that it is worth the effort.
>
> —K. W. Schaie and J. Geiwitz

speed of processing in the elderly. However, there are mitigating factors, which are often overlooked or underestimated. Frequently in laboratory tests, the elderly subject is not allowed adequate time in which to encode and recall information. Restak points out that if elderly subjects are allotted as much time as they need, they often perform at a level that is comparable with younger subjects in terms of recall.

And Daniel A. Walsh (coauthor of "The functional requirement for CD69 in establishment of resident memory CD8+ T cells varies with tissue location" in the *Journal of Immunology Baltimore*, 1950), points out that the level of interest can affect the performance of recall. He reports a study by Irene M. Hulicka in which she tried to teach study participants to associate actual words with nonsense letters. She found that many elderly subjects performed poorly because they refused to learn nonsense words and felt that the task was not worth the effort. When the task was changed to an association of occupational names paired with actual surnames, the elderly performed better. Walsh stresses that laboratory experiments may often be perceived as meaningless and may negatively affect the elderly subjects' performance, while making the task meaningful may positively affect their performance.

One important area of concern is that of neuronal loss due to normal aging. There is no conclusive evidence regarding just how much of the brain is lost with age or just what areas are affected. The interest in neuronal loss may, however, be misdirected. Restak raises some major theoretical issues that are particularly relevant here. He reports on a study comparing the amount of blood flow to and oxygen consumption in the brain in healthy 20-year-old men and healthy 70-year-old men. If there is substantial neuronal loss, there should also be a decrease in blood flow and oxygen consumption. *The results showed that there was no difference between the groups on these measures.*

Redundancy and Plasticity

Restak also points out that even if there were neuronal loss accompanying the aging process, the loss may be offset by the redundancy and plasticity of the brain.

Redundancy implies that there is a greater than necessary number of neurons in the brain, to the extent that neurons may die with no reduction in observed behavior. For instance, we may damage an area of the brain and still show little or no change in our behavior. *Plasticity* refers to the fact that the brain can change in its organization. An area of the brain responsible for a particular function may be damaged, for example, with the result that another area of the brain may take over the function of the damaged area. In this way, as Restak observes, neuronal cell loss due to normal aging may, in fact, lead to greater functioning and more numerous connections in the remaining cells. This suggests that continually using the brain (that is, making more associations) can offset any naturally occurring loss due to cell death. This "use it or lose it" idea is one that we emphasize throughout *Aging Agelessly.*

Of Rats and Responsibility

There is a great deal of literature showing the effect of using the brain on its subsequent development. One study is rather amusing. William T. Greenough (cited in Restak's book) trained rats to reach with a particular paw for pieces of chocolate-chip cookies. Later examination of the area of the brain responsible for motor movement revealed more synaptic connections compared to the brains of untrained rats.

Research also suggests that environment plays a critical role in human development. K.W. Schaie (cited by Restak) conducted a 20-year study of 4,000 people and found that elderly people who maintained active social lives, took on social responsibilities, and accepted new challenges outperformed those who led restricted lives. And by providing mental exercises that engage one's spatial, numerical, and verbal skills, Schaie induced over half of a group of elderly volunteers to improve their performance. He further suggests that memory in the elderly can be improved through the use of mnemonics.

One study on mnemonics in the elderly was conducted by gerontologists E.A. Robertson-Tchabo, C.P. Hausman, and D. Arenberg. In the first phase of the study, elderly subjects were given a list of words to memorize. As expected, initial recall was low. The subjects were shown how to use a particular mnemonic technique while learning lists. With this technique, recall for the lists increased significantly. Days later, however, when they were required to learn and recall a list, performance was again poor. It appeared that the subjects did not spontaneously use the mnemonic technique to help them remember the final list.

In the second phase of the experiment, elderly subjects were divided into three groups, all of whom were required to master a mnemonic technique and apply it to the list learned in the training sessions. During the following session, subjects in all three groups were required to memorize and recall a list of words. The subjects in group 1 were instructed to "use the method we have been using for the past few days." The subjects in group 2 were instructed to form the associations of the mnemonics and to describe verbally the images. The subjects in group 3 were never instructed to apply the mnemonic techniques they had studied.

The results showed that the subjects in group 3 recalled fewer words than those in groups 1 and 2. Interestingly, there was no difference in performance between the subjects in group 1 and group 2. This suggests that mnemonics are valuable aids to memory but that people need to learn how to develop and use them.

Use It or Lose It

This information supports the belief that your memory need not diminish with increasing age. "Use it or lose it" perfectly describes the conclusions reached in scientific literature. By practicing and expanding your mental activities, you can

Brain Flash
Mind Sports Receive Grand Master Status

The mental sport of memory testing and performance has become only the second in the history of mind sports to receive royal sanction for the award of Grand Master titles. The first mind sport to be so honored was chess, when at the St. Petersburg tournament of 1914, Tsar Nicholas II awarded the original Grand Master titles to the five chess greats: Lasker, Capablanca, Alekhine, Tarrasch, and Marshall.

At a formal ceremony organized by the Brain Trust charity on October 26, 1995, Prince Philip of Liechtenstein sanctioned the initial award of Grand Masters of memory to Dominic O'Brien and his great rival Jonathan Hancock, among others. Since then, dozens of individuals of all ages in many countries around the world have claimed the title.

The memory symbol, designed especially for the occasion, combines three elements: the hippocampus, the part of the brain that is responsible for memory; the knight's head over a background globe, linking it through chess to other mind sports worldwide; finally, the horsehead nebula, which is itself a memory trace, an image of an event that transpired in the universe many millions of years ago but is still visible to us.

develop new connections and associations throughout your lifetime. *This finding is extremely relevant to you and your career or business.* All too often seniors in the workplace are seen as incompetent because they can't perform as quickly as younger people. *However, they have a wider range of experience and association than younger, less experienced personnel, and their potential contribution is invaluable.* It is critical to challenge your own mind and the minds of your coworkers, to engage people and keep them involved, and to regularly allow extra time for the elderly. Keep in mind that they are capable of "learning new tricks," provided that they see their relevance, perceive them as worthwhile, and feel motivated.

The Discovery of the Rules of Memory

In his award-winning treatise *The Making of Memory: From Molecules to Mind*, Professor Steven Rose narrates the discovery of the rules of memory by the Greek poet Simonides, who lived around 477 BC.

Simonides' story first appears in *De oratore* ("On the Orator") by the Roman writer and politician Cicero, who relates how Simonides was commissioned to recite a lyric poem in honor of the host of a banquet, the Thessalonian nobleman Scopas. The poem also contained praise for the twin gods Castor and Pollux, which displeased Scopas so much that he would pay Simonides only half his fee, suggesting that he collect the other half from the gods. Later in the banquet, Simonides received a message that two people were waiting to see him. Just after he left the hall, the roof collapsed, killing everyone there and mangling the corpses into an unidentifiable state. The two young men who had summoned Simonides were, of course, Castor and Pollux, taking revenge on Scopas and rewarding Simonides.

The most remarkable part of the story was that Simonides was able to identify the bodies by remembering the sequence in which the guests had been sitting at the banquet table. This experience led Simonides to understand the principles of memory, of which he was supposedly the inventor. He had discovered that the fundamental key to a good memory is the ordered arrangement of the objects to be remembered.

According to Cicero:

He inferred that persons desiring to train this faculty must select places and form mental images of the things they wish to remember and store those images in the places, so that the order of the places will preserve the order of the things, and the images of the things will denote the things themselves. We should then use the places and images respectively, as if they were a wax writing tablet, with the letters written on it.

Sophocles Outwits His Young Son

Sophocles (c. 496–405 BC) is best known as one of the great figures of Greek drama, writing over a hundred works. His greatest masterpiece is the tragedy *Oedipus Tyrannus,* on which Aristotle based his aesthetic theory of drama, and from which Freud derived the name and function of the Oedipus complex. Sophocles was also an outstanding poet, winning first prize 18 times at the Great Dionysia—the most prestigious and important biennial poetry competition in Athens.

What is less well known about Sophocles is that he was also a giant polymath, excelling in a huge variety of fields. In addition to his literary achievements, he was a leading member of the Athenian government as well as being a senior general in the Athenian army. A contemporary parallel would be an amalgam of former US president Barack Obama, playwright David Mamet, and retired US general David Petraeus.

Sophocles lived to a vast age. When Sophocles was in his nineties, his son tried to have him declared mentally incompetent and incapable of managing his own affairs. Sophocles, however, was unwilling to accede. Naturally, he was a wealthy man and his son's demands would have resulted in a substantial transfer of riches, power, and social influence. The situation could not be amicably resolved, so Sophocles' son took him to court, with the aim of publicly proving the decline in his father's mental abilities and wresting control of his affairs from him.

When the case opened, Sophocles conducted his own defense: "Here is the script of a tragedy which I have just completed," he informed the presiding judge. "If you doubt my mental competence, take the script away, and I will recite it in its entirety." His request was granted. When Sophocles reached the second act without having made a single mistake, the case was thrown out of court.

Medieval Memory Theaters

A delightful book on the development of intelligence and memory is *The Day the Universe Changed* by James Burke. It is richly illustrated and gives a pleasant tour through an age that gave rise to the birth of intelligence. We shall now summarize a succinct and entertaining little essay taken from this book, on memory techniques in the Middle Ages, which are still totally valid today.

In a world where few were literate, good memory was essential. For this reason, rhyme, a useful aide-mémoire, was the prevalent form of literature. Up to the fourteenth century, almost everything, except legal documents, was written in rhyme. French merchants used a poem made up of 137 rhyming couplets, which contained all the rules of commercial arithmetic.

Given the cost of writing materials, a trained memory was a necessity for the scholar as much as for the merchant. For more specific tasks than daily recall, medieval professionals used a learning aid that had originally been composed in classical times. The text they learned from was called *Ad Herennium* (written around 86–82 BC by an anonymous teacher of rhetoric in Rome, and named after the dedicatee, one C. Herennius). It was the major mnemonic reference work used in the Middle Ages.

This text provided a technique for recalling vast quantities of material by the use of "memory theaters." The material to be memorized had to be conceived of as a familiar location. This could take the form of a building. If the building was too large, accuracy of recall would suffer. If it was too small, the separate parts of what was to be recalled would be too close to each other for individual recall. If it was too bright, it would blind the memory. Too dark, and it would obscure the material to be remembered.

Each separate part of the location was to be thought of as being about three feet apart so as to keep each major segment of the material isolated from the others. Once the memory theater was prepared in this way, the memorizer would take a mental walk through the building. The route had to be one that was logical and habitual, so that it might be recalled easily and naturally. The theater was now ready to be fitted with the material to be memorized.

The Use of Exaggeration

This material took the form of mental images representing the different elements to be recalled. *Ad Herennium* advised that strong or highly exaggerated images were best. The images should preferably be funny, gaudy, ornamented, unusual, or outrageous. If trying to remember the Queen of Clubs in a card sequence, for instance, you could imagine Queen Elizabeth I swinging a golf club.

These images were to act as "agents" of memory, and each image would trigger recall of several components of the material. If a legal argument were being memorized, for instance, then a dramatic scene might be appropriate. At the relevant point in the journey through the memory theater, this scene would be triggered and played out, reminding the memorizer of the points to be recalled.

The stored images could also relate to individual words, strings of words, or entire arguments. Onomatopoeia (the use of words that sound like the action they describe) was particularly helpful in this regard.

The great medieval theologian St. Thomas Aquinas recommended the theatrical use of imagery for the recall of religious matters. "All knowledge has its origins in sensation," he said. The truth was accessible through visual aids.

As painting and sculpture began to appear in churches, the same techniques for recall were applied. Church imagery took on the form of memory agents. In Giotto's paintings of 1306 on the interior of the Arena Chapel in Padua, the entire series of images is structured as a memory theater. Each Bible story illustrated is told through the medium of a figure or group in a separate place, made more memorable through the use of the recently developed artistic illusion of perspective. The chapel is a mnemonic path to salvation. Cathedrals became enormous memory theaters built to aid the worshippers to recall the details of heaven and hell.

The memory theater is just as valid a technique now as it was in 80 BC, and we advise you to consider its use, in conjunction with Mind Mapping, to increase your own memory skills. Mind Maps also offer a rich field for colorful and outrageous juxtapositions to assist your memory.

Sixty Years of Conducting

One individual who used a similar system and demonstrated its powers over the length of his career was the Italian conductor Arturo Toscanini (1867–1957). He is widely regarded as the greatest orchestral conductor of all time. For more than 60 years, he conducted the world's leading orchestras in a uniquely individual and exciting fashion.

Toscanini's introduction to conducting was sensational: He had trained as a cellist and was touring with an opera company in Brazil in 1886. The Italian musicians had gone on strike against the incompetent local conductor, choosing an Italian replacement. The Brazilian audience took this as a national slur and chased him off. In a situation of complete uproar, Toscanini was asked to step into the breach and overcome the hostility of the crowd (hardly the most auspicious circumstances for any performer). But his surprise debut, at only twenty years of age, received rave reviews from the highly critical local press and was noteworthy for another feat: Tos-

canini conducted the whole piece (Verdi's *Aïda*) without reference to the score, a practice that he retained throughout his
career. After this initial triumph, Toscanini conducted for the
rest of the tour.

Later he admitted to one short memory lapse on that first
tense occasion, but this was very much an exception. The pia-
nist and composer Ferruccio Busoni reported in 1911:

> His memory is a phenomenon in the annals of physiol-
> ogy; but this does not impede his other faculties. . . . He
> had just studied the very difficult score of Dukas's *Ari-
> ane et Barbe-bleue* and the next morning he was going to
> take the first rehearsal—from memory!

Another witness to Toscanini's powers was the famous
composer Igor Stravinsky:

> Conducting an orchestra without the score has become
> the fashion and is often a matter of mere display. There
> is, however, nothing marvelous about this apparent *tour
> de force* . . . one risks little and with a modicum of assur-
> ance and coolness a conductor can easily get away with it.
> It does not really prove that he knows the orchestration
> of the score. But there can be little doubt in the case of
> Toscanini. His memory is proverbial; there is not a detail
> that escapes him, as attendance at one of his rehearsals
> is enough to demonstrate.

The impressions of these two important musical figures are
reinforced by many other stories of Toscanini's memory feats.

There was the famous occasion, for example, when the NBC Symphony Orchestra had scheduled the Prologue to Boito's *Mefistofele*, only to discover the night before rehearsal that the scores for the backstage band had been mislaid. Toscanini simply sat down and wrote them out from memory.

Eye Signals

But why did Toscanini feel the need to conduct without a score in the first place? Undoubtedly because he found it easy to do so, and perhaps also partly because of his short-sightedness, but more importantly because he realized that it enabled him to communicate much more effectively with the orchestra and concentrate on the sound instead of constantly referring to the score. Conductors communicate with musicians not only with their hands, but also with their eyes, and Toscanini wanted to use his eyes to signal key messages to the orchestra. (Remember, eye contact with the audience is also valuable when giving a presentation or lecture.)

Toscanini did not just recall scores parrot-fashion; he also had a clear idea of the exact way the score should sound, and he would fine-tune this with rigorous study of even very familiar pieces before each new performance. His absolute dedication and unrivalled musicianship enabled him to conduct some of the greatest performances of the twentieth century, though he remained a modest man: "I am no genius. I have created nothing. I play the music of other men. I am just a musician."

Toscanini would not accept that in producing a perfect performance of a work, he was in some way interpreting it:

I have often heard people speaking of the *Eroica* of Conductor X, the *Siegfried* of Conductor Y, and the *Aïda* of Conductor Z. And I have always wondered what Beethoven, Wagner, and Verdi would have said about the interpretation of these gentlemen, as if, through them, their works assumed a new paternity. I think that confronted by the *Eroica, Siegfried, Aïda,* an interpreter, entering as deeply as possible into the spirit of the composer, should only be willing to render the *Eroica* of Beethoven, the *Siegfried* of Wagner, and the *Aïda* of Verdi.

Toscanini was also remarkably versatile: he did not merely perform Beethoven, Wagner, Verdi, and other established composers. During his early years as a conductor, he gave world premieres of such famous pieces as Leoncavallo's *I Pagliacci* and Puccini's *La Bohème* and later regularly performed the work of Strauss, Debussy, and Sibelius.

Memory Store

At the end of his career (he was still active at the age of eighty-five), it is estimated that Toscanini had 250 symphonic works, 100 operas, and numerous chamber pieces and songs stored in his memory. Late in life he was challenged to recall from memory some of his own youthful compositions, which he had written sixty or seventy years before and not looked at since. With only a few discrepancies, he remembered them perfectly, text included.

Dominic O'Brien

We have already encountered the eight-time World Memory Champion in chapter 6, where his exploits as winner of the Brain Trust's Brain of the Year Award were briefly chronicled.

At an age (late thirties) when academia tells us that creativity is a thing of the past, Dominic O'Brien decided to master a totally new mental skill and discipline—memory. Within seven years, he had twice won the World Memory Championship, secured the laurels in the World Memory Match Play Championship, written two books on memory, and memorized fifteen full packs of cards (fifty-two cards per pack, shuffled) with no errors, under severe competition conditions, in just one hour! He was recorded in the *Guinness Book of Records* for memorizing a random sequence of fifty-four decks of cards (2,808 playing cards) after looking at each card only once. He was able to correctly recite their order, making only eight errors, four of which he immediately corrected when told he was wrong.

O'Brien became interested in memory in early 1988, when he watched memory expert Creighton Carvello memorize a pack of cards on the British television program *Record Breakers*. Intrigued by this, he sat down with a pack of cards and set about devising his own memory system. His first attempt was far from auspicious: he took twenty-six minutes and made eleven errors. He persisted, however, and it was not long before he could memorize not just one pack of cards, but several. He achieved his first record of six packs at County Sound Radio, Guildford, England, in June 1988.

O'Brien was further motivated by the film *Rain Man*, in which Dustin Hoffman plays an autistic savant with a phenomenal memory. In one scene in the film, Hoffman uses his talent to help his brother (played by Tom Cruise) clean up at the blackjack tables in Las Vegas. This struck O'Brien as a potentially lucrative outlet for his own talent, and he spent the next six months analyzing blackjack and developing his strategy for success. Unfortunately, his meal ticket proved to be a temporary one. Casinos are wise to the techniques of card memorizers, and O'Brien is now banned from most of them.

In 1991 he participated in the first ever World Memory Championship, held at the Athenaeum Club in London. This was organized by the coauthors of this book. In the final, the competitors were lined up head-to-head, and each was given a pack of cards. On Dominic's left was the man who had inspired him to start on a career in memory, Creighton Carvello (whose professional background was in nursing). Dominic began to deal, turning the cards over faster and faster, until Creighton lost his concentration. O'Brien won the event and assumed the title of World Memory Champion.

O'Brien does not recognize any limits to the potential of human memory and has continued to improve on his records and set ever more impressive ones. His achievements include memorization of a pack of cards in fifty-five seconds, fifty-four packs of cards, the entire set of Trivial Pursuit questions, and pi to 22,500 digits (breaking the Guinness World Record for that feat in 1998).

The mathematical symbol pi (the ratio of the circumference of a circle to its diameter) has exerted a fascination over mathematicians for millennia. Pi, which starts 3.1415926..., is a transcendental number, which means that it continues indefinitely without ever dissolving into a repetitive sequence of digits. As such, it is an excellent tool for memory tests. O'Brien set the record for memorizing pi and set his sights on improving it to 50,000 digits. Rajveer Meena currently holds the record at 70,000. This is a phenomenal amount of information to store in the memory; just to read out 50,000 digits at the rate of one per second would take over 14 hours.

Brain Flash
Memory Training: A Cure for Blocked Brains

O'Brien's feats should serve as inspiration for anyone who wants to use his or her brain more efficiently. After all, in an age of motorized transport, being able to run short distances very quickly is not a socially useful skill, but that does not prevent us from wanting to keep fit or from marveling at the achievements of marathon stars. Everyone who feels their brain may have become slightly flabby and who is daunted at the prospect of, for example, learning a new language should take inspiration from O'Brien's achievements. Training your memory is a form of aerobics for the mind, which is especially vital as you age.

What Should I Do Now?

1. Absorb the message contained in the medieval memory theater and classical memory techniques, such as the Roman room, as explained in this chapter.

2. Use the colorful, dramatic, and visual impact of Mind Maps to help yourself remember key lists, ideas, and facts.

3. Begin by making a conscious effort to remember the names of people to whom you are introduced at meetings or parties. Try to link their appearance with their name, or find out one singular and memorable fact about them that will aid your recall.

4. Move on to memorizing information in books, then progress to new mind sports and languages, and gradually become more ambitious!

CHAPTER 12

Profiles in Ageless Aging

*If I had my life to live over again, I would have made
a rule to read some poetry and listen to some music at
least once a week for, perhaps, the parts of my brain now
atrophied would thus have been kept active through use.*
—CHARLES DARWIN

We have so far covered the theory, the physiology, and the philosophy of improving with age and have set you various challenges and provided you with stimulation to assist you as you progress through life. Now we turn to examples of those who are challenging themselves, with brief profiles of modern, living people who started out with no special advantages in life but have found ways of giving themselves fresh challenges as they age. By doing this, they nurture extra synaptic connections and keep themselves mentally alert.

Some of these people have already achieved extraordinary heights in later life; others are taking the preparatory steps to launch themselves into their golden age. In this chapter we deliberately avoid historical geniuses and intellectual superstars to demonstrate that anyone can substantially improve their prognosis, using the strategy we outline.

Renegades from the Norm

All of us know people who contradict the normal negative stereotypes associated with aging. These renegades from the norm are intelligent, active, ambitious, inquisitive, stimulating, and fun to be with. The word *renegade* is particularly appropriate, for it comes from *run-a-gate*, meaning *one who has escaped*. These individuals have escaped from the downward curve of the mental aptitude norm.

Brain Flash
Still Cooking at Eighty-Five

Nana Yousif is a self-taught cook who began her career in the kitchen at the age of 18, but she never bothered to write down any of her recipes. Now, those recipes are being captured digitally via YouTube and TikTok videos thanks to her loving and dedicated assistant (and granddaughter) Dina Ibrahim.

As of last count, Nana and Dina reported having 260,000 YouTube subscribers, 537,000 TikTok followers, and 64,000 Instagram followers. Yousif loves watching YouTube cooking videos from all over the world, which gave Dina the idea for their show: *Nana's Kitchen.*

According to Dina, Nana moves so quickly in the kitchen that she and her cousin find it challenging to keep up with her during the filming.

—CTV News, Calgary

In this chapter we not only profile notable examples of people who refuse to "wind down" but also show the measures being taken by those in a younger age group to challenge themselves in true Goethean style as an effective weapon against the encroaching years. Such measures include starting up entirely new careers or businesses well after the age of conventional retirement; acquiring awe-inspiring new mental skills; striving for extraordinary artistic goals; and, on a personal level, setting oneself extreme self-challenges of physical and mental endurance.

One technique used by coauthor Ray Keene to stretch his mental capacities is regularly (at least twice a month) to take on up to forty opponents at chess at one and the same time. His adversaries in such displays are not restricted to weak pushovers, but standardly include former British champions and players who have earned the title of international master. Ray's best exploit so far (which he claims as a world percentage and speed record) was to win 101 games, draw 5, and lose 1 in just three hours. After such displays he stretches himself even further by showing the moves of all the games, *from memory*, to the participants.

At the age of fifty-three, coauthor Tony Buzan set himself the task of mastering the fiendishly difficult Japanese board game go. Statisticians have calculated that go is infinitely more involved than chess in the sheer number of possible moves. Yet in the space of a mere eight months, Tony raised his skills in the game to near black-belt level, from where he could seriously challenge Western champions and high-level Japanese players.

Now let us see how a variety of people over a broad canvas are challenging and reinventing themselves, like that mythical bird, the golden phoenix, as they age. Such people maintain, and even extend, their mental fitness, strength, and alertness.

Frank Felberbaum (Aged eighty-six)

While writing this chapter, we spoke to one of the international brain stars of memory, Frank Felberbaum, of the Felberbaum Consulting Group Inc. Memory Training Systems. Here are his thoughts on the aging brain as it affects him and on what he is doing to challenge himself:

1. As you age, you can *expand your brain*, just as you *expand a business*.

2. The aging brain loves newness and the exotic. The renegade from the norm is the older person who can easily adapt to change, likes learning new things, and enjoys going to new places. Sometimes living with someone who has these characteristics can produce the same benefits.

3. Just as it used to be important to have the right connections to succeed in business and life, so now it is necessary to make the right connections to keep your aging brain successful.

4. Memory is a conscious, proactive creative process. If we control that process, we can control our memory and thus keep the aging brain young and vital.

5. The mind has to be jolted by absurdity, even though it seeks the familiar. Change is difficult but highly necessary to survive and enjoy aging.

6. If a young person makes an error in memory, it is usually attributed to information overload. If, however, an older person has a memory failure, the reason given is usually aging. In most situations, the older individual just needs a little more time to respond with the same accuracy as the younger individual.

These points focus on my impressions of why the brain gets better as it gets older. The following is what I know about my own improving brain and memory.

Since I am constantly training thousands of executives, managers, sales reps, and technical staff in hundreds of corporations, I am constantly and consciously aware of my brain and memory and how and why it functions as it does.

I am aware of the methods and techniques that I use and of the effort I expend to achieve my memory success and that of my many memory-workshop participants. This has kept my mind razor-sharp! I have been a professional in the corporate memory development arena for over twenty-eight years and have never reached a plateau. I have trained my brain and memory to seek challenges and continuously learn new and stimulating ideas, concepts, and skills. My prime objective for my clients and myself is to prevent business information loss, hence the name of my training program, the Business of Memory. What we learn takes a lifetime to acquire and an equal amount of energy, and it is too valuable to allow it to become part of the great disappearing act. Because of my unquenchable thirst for new knowledge about the brain and memory, it is digesting anything in its path. I can't wait to arise each morning to think, to learn, and to teach.

Edith Murway-Traina (Aged 101)

In September 2021, *People* magazine featured a story about 100-year-old Edith Murway-Traina—the Guinness World Records' oldest competitive powerlifter.

Murway-Traina, a former dance instructor, started going to the gym just a few years ago in response to a friend's invitation, where she discovered her passion for pumping iron. "Going on a regular basis," she said, "I found that I was enjoying it, and I was challenging myself to get a little bit better and a little bit better. Before long, I was part of the team." Not long after she started, she was entering weightlifting competitions . . . and winning!

Murway-Traina credits her success to her passion and persistence. Sometimes she's tired and doesn't feel like going to the gym, but she fights through it and usually enjoys the workout. Her strength trainer, Bill Berkley, is amazed, "It is such a challenge and to do it at that level at that age is mind-blowing."

Calvin Roberts (Aged sixty-six)

How old is too old to play professional basketball in the National Basketball Association (NBA)? If history is any indication, the answer to that question appears to be the mid-forties. Nat Hickey was the oldest at forty-five. As head coach for the Providence Steamrollers during the 1947–48 season, he activated himself as a player for two games—evidence that people can still be creative (and cunning) well past their supposed peak.

Calvin Roberts hopes to unseat Hickey as the oldest NBA player ever, and he claims to be in better shape now than he was when he was drafted by the San Antonio Spurs in 1980. He didn't make the team at that time, but he went on to play for nearly twenty years overseas, officially retiring in 1999. Like many retirees, however, he was far from done.

Brain Flash
Age-Old Wisdom on the Bench

Sir Frederick Lawton, a Lord Justice of Appeal, 1972–86, says it would be wrong to ban judges over sixty-five. The older the judge, the better he or she is likely to be.

"There is a saying among judges that during his first five years of appointment, the newcomer to the Bench should remember that he knows little about his job and that during the next five years he thinks he knows a lot but doesn't. It is only after ten years that he can consider himself reasonably competent. A judge appointed in his early fifties, as most judges are, would not be on top of his work until he was over sixty and in sight of retirement at sixty-five.

"The conscientious judge—and most are—is aware that he learns more about his job every day he sits. He never stops learning. Time and time again he says to himself, after making a decision with which he is not entirely satis-fied, 'I'll never do that again.' As the years go by, the mem-ory acquires a larger and larger store of judicial 'don'ts.' Providing a judge has good health, particularly good mental health, he is likely to become a better judge as he gets older. The two best judges in my professional lifetime, Lord Reid and Lord Denning, both delivered some of their best judgments when well into their seventies. What a loss to jurisprudence there would have been, had they been obliged to retire at sixty-five.

"As Lord Justice of Appeal, I had the privilege of sitting with Lord Denning. I was sixty when I went to the Court of Appeal. I had been a High Court judge for eleven years. Lord Denning was about sixty-eight. Every time I sat with him, I learned more about judging."

—The Times

In response to his wife's encouragement to get back in shape so he could play with their children, Roberts started working out again. When he felt he was back into his college shape, everything clicked, and he felt great. He continued to push himself harder until he felt he was in even better condition than when he played at California State University at Fullerton, where he once played against Magic Johnson.

Roberts ramped up his workouts, lifted heavier weights, and played ball at a local YMCA in Las Vegas. As he gained confidence, he started sending letters to NBA teams letting them know that he was ready and eager for a tryout and requesting an opportunity to prove himself in the NBA Summer League in Las Vegas.

Now a father of five and grandfather of two, Roberts is still waiting for an answer. He never received an invitation to play in the Summer League, but he attended the games as a spectator so he could get his head into it—watching and listening to the players and coaches.

Anyone else may have been frustrated and discouraged, but Roberts maintains an upbeat attitude. "As long as I'm in physically good shape and I can rebound, jump, shoot, and everything, I fulfilled my part," Roberts says, and he continues to work toward achieving his dream. After all, it's that competitive drive that's keeping him fit, both physically and mentally.

Jeff Bezos (Aged fifty-eight)

Jeff Bezos started Amazon.com in 1994. He was in his thirties at the time. It began as an online bookstore and has grown to carry nearly every imaginable product—a shopper's paradise that Bezos initially conceived as the "everything store." The company's success may be attributed to the fact that, like its founder, it never stops growing and improving. Since its beginning, the company has expanded into a variety of industries, including entertainment (Prime Video), cloud computing, and artificial intelligence (Alexa), and it has its sights on more, including groceries, home improvement, business lending, pharmaceuticals, and industrial supplies.

One of the richest entrepreneurs on the planet, Bezos is committed to staying young forever. He's a well-known physical fitness buff who looks younger than his age. But looking young isn't enough: he wants to stay young, and he's investing heavily in medical research and technologies to discover how to slow, stop, and reverse the aging process.

Bezos keeps his mind sharp by staying hungry, thinking big, and tackling challenges that he's passionate about, such as interrupting the aging process and colonizing remote planets. In 2000, he secretly founded Blue Origin, a private space exploration company, to pursue his dreams of exploring deep space and colonizing other planets as a backup option for earth. In July 2021, he went to space and back on an eleven-minute ride aboard the rocket and capsule system developed by Blue Origin engineers. Accompanying him on his journey were his brother, Mark; Wally Funk, an eighty-two-year-old pilot and one of the Mercury 13 women who trained for NASA's Mercury program but was never given the opportunity to go into space; and an eighteen-year-old high-school graduate named Oliver Daemen, who was Blue Origin's first paying customer and whose father, an investor, purchased his ticket.

Bezos prioritizes sleep, sleeping eight hours per night to boost his energy and mood. He schedules his "high IQ meetings" at 10 a.m., after breakfast and before lunch. If anything comes up in the late afternoon, he holds off on convening a meeting until the next day. "Eight hours of sleep makes a big difference for me, and I try hard to make that a priority," Bezos told *Thrive Global* in November 2016. "For me, that's the needed amount to feel energized and excited."

Brain Flash
Lack of Ability or Motivation?

According to Dr. Owen Anderson, an American physiologist who publishes *Running Research News*, loss of determination has a greater influence on declining performance than age itself.

"We used to think that, at thirty-five or so, athletes began a steady physiological decline, but now we are finding out that most of what we thought was an age-related decline is due to reduction in training," Anderson said. "We are finding that runners who are able to continue their training with intense workouts do not lose much between twenty-five and forty-five.

"At forty-five, your race times may be slower; but it is not the aging process that has given you leaden legs. It is probably reduced motivation, a reduction in quality training, and lack of consistency of training."

Professor Benjamin Zander (Aged eighty-three)

A new force has entered the brain research arena: the force of music.

Benjamin Zander founded the Boston Philharmonic Orchestra in 1979 and has appeared as a guest conductor with orchestras around the world. Since early in his career, he has been on a mission to "musicate the world."

Over the course of twenty-five years, Zander collaborated with the London-based Philharmonia Orchestra on eleven recordings, including a nearly complete cycle of Mahler symphonies as well as symphonies of Bruckner and Beethoven. *High Fidelity* magazine named their recording of Mahler's Sixth Symphony "The Best Classical Recording" of 2002; their Mahler Third was awarded "Critic's Choice" by the German Record Critics' Award Association; and their Mahler Ninth and Bruckner Fifth recordings were nominated for Grammy awards for Best Orchestral Performance. As part of his commitment to musicating the world, Zander included an audio explanation as a separate disk with each of his Philharmonia recordings.

In 2012, Zander founded the Boston Philharmonic Youth Orchestra (BPYO), which draws young musicians aged twelve to twenty-one from the entire northeastern US to its weekly rehearsals and performances in Boston Symphony Hall. This tuition-free orchestra tours regularly and has performed in Carnegie Hall, Amsterdam's Concertgebouw, and the Berlin Philharmonie, among many other renowned halls. In the summer of 2017 the BPYO toured South America. Their 2018 tour included performances of Mahler's Ninth Symphony in eight European cities. In 2019, the BPYO did a tour around Brazil with resounding success.

Zander led the New England Conservatory Youth Philharmonic on fifteen international tours and made several documentaries for the Public Broadcasting Service (PBS). His interpretation classes, "Interpretations of Music: Lessons for

Life," have been viewed online by tens of thousands of people around the world. In 2018, the Benjamin Zander Center was established to support this dimension of his career. Through an immersive multimedia platform, the Center provides comprehensive access to all aspects of Zander's musical work.

In 2019, Zander was presented with a Lifetime Achievement Award at the ABSA Achievement Awards in Johannesburg in recognition of his contributions in music, culture, and leadership. His TED talk, "The Transformative Power of Classical Music," has been seen by over twenty million people.

Brain Flash
True Works of Genius

"I hold that of all Verdi's operas, only *Otello* and *Falstaff* are truly works of genius."   —Bernard Levin

Verdi wrote *Otello* in 1887, at the age of 74, and *Falstaff* in 1893, at the age of 80. They were the last two of his numerous operas.

The Effect of Music on IQ

Many scientists now believe that listening to certain types of music can make people more intelligent.

University of California physicist Gordon L. Shaw examined brain responses during abstract reasoning tasks and found a pattern of activity resembling that of music. Together with psychologist Frances Rauscher (a former professional cellist), he attempted to establish whether providing music training to young children could improve their spatial reasoning skills. The initial results were extremely positive: after three, six and nine months of lessons, the children's abstract reasoning showed great improvement. This was the only aspect that showed such improvement, suggesting that music was not simply attracting their attention but training their brains.

Improved IQ for the Older Age Group

Encouraged by these results, Shaw and Rauscher decided to analyze what happens to adults when they listen to music. They compared three listening states: a Mozart piano sonata, a relaxation tape, and silence, and tested spatial reasoning after each. Their results revealed that Mozart had an extremely positive effect.

What about other forms of music? Can listening to heavy metal, acid rock, or rap music have the same stimulating effect as Mozart? Shaw and Rauscher believe not, since these forms of music do not have the required structural and harmonic complexity. Shaw claims:

> We are born with some of the structure, there are certain natural patterns that can be excited, and when we hear Mozart's music it is pleasing for us, because these natural patterns are being excited in our brain while we listen.

The experiments of Shaw and Rauscher indicated that similar patterns of brainwave were occurring while listening to Mozart and while playing chess.

> ### Brain Flash
> ### Role Model
>
> Toscanini's pupil, the late conductor Sir Georg Solti, who was 82 at the peak of his career, was one of the driving forces behind the Verdi Festival, organized by London's Royal Opera House. In an interview on June 10, 1995, on the eve of his stupendous performance of *La Traviata*, Sir Georg announced his ambition to become the world's first active conductor at the age of 100.
>
> *La Traviata* was performed during a heat wave which had London sweltering. Sir Georg's sole concession to the freak temperatures was to remove his jacket: "The first time I ever did this in my life."
>
> Unfortunately, he fell short of his goal, passing away on September 5, 1997, at the age of eighty-five.

Rikki Hunt (Aged sixty-eight)

Rikki Hunt, Mind Mapper and CEO of Rikki Hunt Associates Ltd., which delivers entrepreneurial coaching and consulting to the private and public sectors, is known as the originator of "the thinking organization." He challenges himself to achieve his potential by climbing mountains, such as the Eiger, the Matterhorn, and Everest, and by walking to the North Pole.

Ask yourself which other group of human beings the renegades in this chapter most closely resemble. The answer? Children!

And what do all the poets, philosophers, religious leaders, and thinkers, in their various ways, say must be the impetus for the aging human? "Except ye . . . become as little children,

---

Brain Flash
Don't Say *Can't*

Rikki Hunt is terrified of heights. But the summer of 1995 saw him scaling the leafy peaks of the Eiger and the Matterhorn. Why? To prove to his staff that anyone can do anything, given time and dedication.

Three juggling balls are displayed in Hunt's office in Swindon. Hunt cannot juggle but they are there to remind him he can learn to do so if he chooses.

"I believe very strongly that people can do anything they want," he says. "After years of being kicked down I have a life quest to teach people to realize their potential. There is no limit, and that is why our company slogan is: Don't say can't."

—Personnel Today

---

ye shall not enter into the kingdom of heaven" (Matthew 18:3).

Or, as William Blake would have put it, "You must leave the age of innocence (childhood), enter the age of experience (early middle age), and reenter the age of innocence (advanced childhood), if you are to enter paradise."

What Should I Do Now?

1. Start listening to classical music to harmonize the full flow of your intelligence. Mozart, Haydn, Bach, Beethoven, Mahler, and Stravinsky are particularly recommended.

2. Dream up an ambitious but realistic new challenge for yourself—and achieve it. It could be professional, cultural, or personal (for example, a sport or hobby).

3. Rely on yourself. Don't wait for others to help you or do it for you.

4. Remember Goethe's message from chapter 5: "In the beginning was the deed. . . . Begin it now."

Brain Flash

Seventy-Four-Year-Old Fitness Fanatic

A 2019 article in *Shape* magazine told how Joan MacDonald overcame multiple health conditions by adopting a disciplined workout routine.

At seventy years old, she was taking several medications for high blood pressure, high cholesterol, and acid reflux. Her doctor informed her that her health was failing and that she would need to up her dosages unless she made drastic changes to her lifestyle. "I knew I had to do something different," MacDonald told *Shape*. "I had watched my mom go through the same thing, taking medication after medication, and I didn't want that life for myself."

With the help of her daughter Michelle, a yogi, competitive power lifter, professional chef, and owner of Tulum Strength Club in Mexico, McDonald started walking, practicing yoga, and lifting weights. Initially, she struggled to lift even a ten-pound weight, and she would work out only as much as her body could tolerate, but she eventually progressed to spending two hours in the gym, five days a week. "I'm very slow, so it takes me almost double the time to finish a regular workout," said MacDonald.

MacDonald attributes her success to having a consistent workout routine and getting it "out of the way" first thing in the morning, at about 7 a.m.

CHAPTER 13

Evaluating Your Brain's Health and Fitness

What can the average person do to strengthen his or her mind? The important thing is to be actively involved in areas unfamiliar to you.
—ARNOLD SCHEIBEL, HEAD OF BRAIN RESEARCH INSTITUTE, UCLA

We have now seen a group of people, renegades from the norm, challenging themselves and extending their mental vistas. In this chapter, we provide a smorgasbord of mental tests, self-checks, fitness gauges, and new parameters to explore how fit your brain really is.

We explain how mind sports and brain calisthenics can keep your brain fit as you age. We quote research from the University of California at Irvine indicating that mind sports may help prevent Alzheimer's disease by building new brain circuitry.

Is your brain fit? Is there room for improvement, and, if so, how much? Later in this chapter, you can test yourself in the areas of self and time management, the physical brain, emotional stability, sensual awareness, memory, and creativity—and find out!

Brain Flash
Seize Your Opportunities

Running a big business is like playing a game of chess: it requires vast logical analysis and the courage to seize opportunities.   —*The Sunday Times*

The Benefits of Mind Sports and Physical Sports

Chess is the gymnasium of the mind.

—V.I. LENIN

I strongly approve of rational games,
for they serve to perfect the art of thinking.

—GOTTFRIED WILHELM LEIBNIZ

Guru Hargobind (fl. 16th c.), Sixth Guru of the Sikhs, encouraged
his followers to look to physical fitness, to learn martial arts,
and to become expert horsemen to protect the rights of themselves
and others. Sikhs were to be "Sant Sipa"—Saint Soldiers.

—THE TIMES

Chess: King of Western Mind Sports

Why are mind games, and chess in particular, regarded as important? The answer is that, throughout the history of culture, prowess at mind games has been associated with intelligence. Mind sports play a vital part in the lives of many geniuses, and of the various Western mind sports, chess is undoubtedly king. It is the one practiced most widely and has the best-documented theory to back it up. A number of geniuses have rated chess highly. Goethe called the game "the touchstone of the intellect." Haroun al-Rashid, the Abbasid caliph of Islam (AD c.763–809), idealized in the *Arabian Nights,* was the first of his dynasty to play chess.

The eleventh-century Byzantine emperor Alexius Comnenus was allegedly playing chess when he was surprised by a murderous conspiracy, which, being a good chess player, he naturally managed to escape!

One if the best ways to challenge your mind through chess is to solve winning-move puzzles, which are readily available online; just search the web for "chess puzzles."

Brain Flash
It's Never Too Late

What can the average person do to strengthen his or her mind? The important thing is to be actively involved in areas unfamiliar to you. Anything that's intellectually challenging can probably serve as a kind of stimulus for dendritic growth, which means it adds to the computation reserves in your brain.

Do puzzles; try a musical instrument; repair something; try the arts; dance; date provocative people; try tournament bridge, chess; even sailboat racing. And remember, researchers agree that it's never too late. All of life should be a learning experience because we are challenging our brain and therefore building brain circuitry. Literally, this is the way the brain operates.

—Arnold Scheibel, head of the Brain Research Institute, UCLA, Los Angeles

The Aladdin of the fairy tale was, in real life, a chess player, a lawyer from Samarkand in the court of Tamerlaine. Tamerlaine himself, the conqueror of half the known world during the fourteenth century, loved to play chess and named his son Shah Rukh, since Tamerlaine was moving a rook at the time the birth was announced.

Another genius, Benjamin Franklin, was an enthusiastic chess player. Indeed, the first chess publication in America was Franklin's *Morals of Chess,* which appeared in 1786. Chess was mentioned by Shakespeare, Goethe, Leibniz, and Einstein; Tsar Ivan the Terrible, Queen Elizabeth I, Catherine the Great, and Napoleon all prided themselves on their chess skills.

Here and now, we show you how to develop your own mental qualities, following the example of chess and other mind sports champions.

The Growth of Mind Sports

Since the dawn of civilization some 10,000 years ago, history has recorded humans playing games. The earliest writings of ancient civilizations refer to games similar to tic-tac-toe. As a civilization progressed, so did the complexity of its games.

The development of games over the centuries has been a fascinating one. It has now reached a point that will lead to an evolutionary change in the way in which we engage in combat, entertain ourselves, and think about our intelligence.

International Brain Stars

A measure of the growth of interest in mind sports is reflected in the increased prize fund for major contests. In 1969 the World Chess Championship match was worth around 3,000 rubles (less than $3,000) to the winner. In 1990 Garry Kasparov and Anatoly Karpov contested a purse of $2 million. The prize fund has changed little since that time: the 2021 championship between the reigning world champion Magnus Carlsen and challenger Ian Nepomniachtchi was played for a €2 million ($2,064,460) prize fund.

Concurrent with the explosion of interest in chess and mind sports has come a similar explosion of interest in measuring general mental skills, competing in them, and forming organizations based on them. Witness the dramatic growth of Mensa, whose membership in England alone increases by over 2,000 per year. Members' major hobbies include chess and other mind sports and solving mental puzzles. Similarly, we have witnessed the growing popularity of the International Brain Bee (thebrainbee.org). The Brain Bee was founded by Dr. Norbert Myslinski at the University of Maryland as a neuroscience competition for high-school students. Thanks to extraordinary volunteer commitments of time and resources, it has grown from a grassroots effort to a successful global educational and outreach initiative.

Mental world records are analogous to physical world records. They include memorizing tens of thousands of decimal digits in the number pi, the fastest speed for the memorization of playing cards, the highest IQs, top chess ratings, and other mental feats accomplished either inside or outside the course of formal competitions. Various organizations and their panels of experts give official authorization and recognition to such records.

This growth of interest in the mental arena has become all-pervasive. Local, national, and international competitions proliferate: virtually all major newspapers and magazines carry articles and columns and even feature sections on chess, bridge, and brain twisters. In past years, the Tournament of the Mind in the London *Times* and the *Mastermind* program on BBC television have attracted large followings. Hundreds of competitors descend on towns and cities for chess, bridge, go, Scrabble, Monopoly, and other championships, and the demand for literature, clubs, playing venues, and competitions steadily increases.

Evidence is growing that the dominance of physical sports as the more popular medium of human expression over mental sports reflects not an innate preference but simply the lack of opportunity to express an equal, if not greater, interest in the mental arena. With the growth of information technology and electronic data systems, we have reached a point when, for the first time, competition on the mental battlefield can be seen instantaneously by as many spectators as competitions on sports grounds. World Chess Championship matches are being transmitted to billions of viewers worldwide via online and cable networks.

This global interest in mental world championship contests can be seen as the result of a natural interest by the human mind in its own function and the way in which it can develop games to test its limits. The phenomenon is common to all games, as the statistics on those interested in the different mental arenas more than adequately prove.

Pumping Up Your Brain Power

A study reported in the journal *Nature* shows that both physical and mental exercise can keep the brain sharp into old age. It might help prevent Alzheimer's disease and other mental disorders that accompany aging. The study, by Carl Cotman of the University of California at Irvine, is the first to show a direct link between physical and mental activity, demonstrating that growth factors in the brain can be controlled by exercise. There is already a great deal of evidence to suggest that those who exercise regularly live longer and score higher marks in mental tests. Cotman's findings add important weight to the necessity for physical activity to combat the aging process. According to Cotman, "The brain really is a muscle. When you exercise it, the mind grows and is capable of handling more projects and complex problems."

Cotman used rodents in his research, as rats have similar exercise habits to humans. The rats were allowed to regulate their exercise, and each demonstrated a unique preference. Some were lazy "couch" rats, rarely getting on the treadmill, while others were "runaholics," running obsessively for hours every night. Those that exercised showed much higher levels of brain-derived neurotrophic factor (BDNF), an important growth factor in the brain.

It appears that there is an ideal threshold of exercise that provides the maximum possible benefit. Cotman's results demonstrated that the rats that exercised excessively showed no better growth than those that exercised around the optimum level.

Slimming to Success

Meanwhile, a Canadian study has found that obesity can cause sleep disturbances, which may lead to learning disorders and a significant drop in IQ. Susan Rhodes, a psychologist at the Medical University of South Carolina in Charleston, claims that obesity causes a decrease of oxygen in the brain during sleep due to fat in the throat or to a more indirect means involving the central nervous system, leading to a type of brain damage. She also suggests that putting the obese on diets may reverse the damage and "make them smarter."

Finally, remember: if you are trying to develop a challenging new mental skill, such as Mind Mapping, chess, or go, or are trying to improve your diet or give up smoking, refer back to our vitally important section in chapter 4 on transforming a Big Bad Habit into a Good New Habit. Metapositive thinking is the way to change yourself for the better, and you cannot start soon enough. This is a key component of the strategy for successful aging.

Brain Flash
Research Shows the Mind Is Capable
of Growth in Old Age

Researchers can now demonstrate that certain crucial areas of human intelligence do not decline in old age among people who are generally healthy.

The new research challenges beliefs long held both by scientists and the public and suggests that, among people who remain physically and emotionally healthy, some of the most important forms of intellectual growth can continue well into the eighties. It also suggests that decline in intelligence can be reversed in some instances and that earlier notions about the loss of brain cells, as a person ages, were in error.

Countless intellectually vigorous lives may have atrophied on the mistaken assumption that old age brings an unavoidable mental deterioration.

"The expectation of a decline is a self-fulfilling prophecy," said Werner Schaie, a researcher on aging. "Those who don't accept the stereotype of a helpless old age, but instead feel they can do as well in old age as they have at other times in their lives, don't become ineffective before their time."

—*The International Herald Tribune*

How Fit Is Your Brain?

What sort of shape is your brain in? The following questionnaire tests your brain power. Identify your strengths and the areas that need improvement.

Circle a number for each answer, and then note your total score for each section.

Self and Time Management	Yes	Not Sure/ Sometimes	No
1. Do you have a clear vision of what you want from life?	2	1	0
2. Do you burden yourself with more than fifty pages of "to do" notes?	0	1	2
3. Are you punctual?	2	1	0
4. Do you use images, symbols, and colors in your diary?	2	1	0
5. Do you regularly feel stressed?	0	1	2
6. Do you like planning?	2	1	0
7. Do you plan regular holidays and breaks for yourself?	2	1	0
8. Do you feel guilty if you're not working?	0	1	2
9. Do you remember your life in individual years?	2	1	0
10. Do your regularly review your life?	2	1	0
11. Do you generally look forward to tomorrow?	2	1	0
12. Do you feel threatened by your diary?	0	1	2

The Physical Brain	Yes	Not Sure/ Sometimes	No
1. Do you eat (and like) lots of sugar and/or salt?	0	1	2
2. Do you regularly eat fresh vegetables and fruit?	2	1	0
3. Do you eat a lot of refined foods?	0	1	2
4. Are you considerably over- or underweight?	0	1	2
5. Do you exercise regularly and enjoy it?	2	1	0
6. Do you have regular health checks?	2	1	0
7. Do you drink excessively?	0	1	2
8. Do you regularly take drugs of any sort?	0	1	2
9. Do you grill rather than fry foods?	2	1	0
10. Do you have a varied diet?	2	1	0
11. Do you drink more than six cups of tea and/ or coffee per day?	0	1	2
12. Are you a smoker?	0	1	2

Emotional Stability	Yes	Not Sure/ Sometimes	No
1. Are you self-confident?	2	1	0
2. Are you able to cry?	2	1	0
3. Do you often get annoyed?	0	1	2
4. Do people generally consider you a happy person?	2	1	0
5. Do you maintain friendships for a long time?	2	1	0
6. Do you often feel helpless?	0	1	2
7. Is life often a burden?	0	1	2
8. Do you get along with your family?	2	1	0
9. Do you say what you feel?	2	1	0
10. Do you like to touch and be touched?	2	1	0
11. Do you feel happy when others feel happy?	2	1	0
12. Do you generally keep your fears to yourself?	0	1	2

Sensual Awareness	Yes	Not Sure/ Sometimes	No
1. Do you enjoy dancing?	2	1	0
2. Do you regularly enjoy films, plays, paintings, and music?	2	1	0
3. Are you able to recall visual information clearly?	2	1	0
4. Are you able to recall smells and tastes clearly?	2	1	0
5. Do you recall sounds, tactile sensations, and physical movements clearly?	2	1	0
6. Do you eat to live, not live to eat?	0	1	2
7. Are you sensual?	2	1	0
8. Do you enjoy playing with children?	2	1	0
9. Do you like your body?	2	1	0
10. Do you like nature?	2	1	0
11. Do others consider you well-dressed?	2	1	0
12. Do you dislike driving?	0	1	2

Memory Test 1: Long-Term Memory

On a piece of paper, write down the names of the planets of the solar system, in order of distance from the sun (closest first).

1. _____
2. _____
3. _____
4. _____
5. _____
6. _____
7. _____
8. _____

Memory Test 2: Recall during Learning

Read through the following list of words once, and then carry out the instruction that follows:

1. cage	9. of	17. the	25. will
2. exact	10. the	18. wood	26. afraid
3. his	11. the	19. door	27. join
4. pan	12. of	20. glass	28. ceiling
5. foot	13. wide	21. of	29. top
6. page	14. Leonardo da Vinci	22. of	30. finger
7. high	15. rainy	23. turn	31. fire
8. and	16. tiny	24. up	

Without looking at the words again, write down as many as you can remember on a piece of paper and then refer to the scoring.

Creativity

Before proceeding, make sure that you have a pen and pencil and a watch so that you can time yourself for a minute. Then do the following:

Write down, in one minute, as fast as you can, all the uses you can possibly think of for an elastic band.

How Fit Is Your Brain? Answers

SELF AND TIME MANAGEMENT

Scoring

18–24: Excellent. You are working at something like maximum efficiency.

12–17: Good, but there is plenty of room for improvement.

6–11: Could (and should) try harder.

0–5: You are not using anything like the full power of your brain and body.

THE PHYSICAL BRAIN

Scoring

18–24: Excellent. You are giving your brain every opportunity to flourish.

12–17: Good, but you may not be looking after yourself quite as well as you think.

6–11: You may be losing out mentally by underestimating the importance of physical health to a sharp mind.

0–5: You are undermining your brain power by bodily abuse. Give your brain a chance.

EMOTIONAL STABILITY

Scoring

18–24: You are unusually mature emotionally.

12–17: You are generally mature but would benefit from working on this area.

6–11: You undervalue yourself—wrongly.

0–5: Pay attention to this aspect of your mind.

SENSUAL AWARENESS

Scoring

18–24: Excellent. You live a well-balanced, sensual, cultural, and physical life, and your brain benefits as a result.

12–17: A good score, on which you would do well to build.

6–11: An average score, but not a particularly good one. Remember that there is more to thinking than dry theorizing.

0–5: You are in danger of starving your brain of stimulation. Enjoy yourself!

MEMORY TEST 1

Answer:

Mercury, Venus, Earth, Mars, Jupiter, Saturn, Uranus, Neptune, Pluto. Score one point for each planet that you placed correctly.

Scoring:

8–9: Exceptional

6–7: Very good and well above average

4–5: Still above average

2–3: Average to just above average

1–2: Surprisingly, quite normal

The reason for the generally low score on a subject such as this, to which our brains have been exposed in both school and general life, is that we have not been trained to use our long-term memories.

MEMORY TEST 2

Scoring:

You will probably find that you recalled at least one of the words that were repeated (*of, the*), that you remembered *Leonardo da Vinci* (because it stood out) and that, of all the other words, you remembered more from the beginning and end, plus words from the middle that were in some way associated with each other or meant something special to you. If you remembered all the words, you have an exceptionally well-trained memory. If not, don't worry. But if you think that remembering such a list is completely beyond your capabilities, you are wrong. Study the methods in this book, and you will find that you can.

CREATIVITY

Scoring:

The normal score on this creativity test, based on the work of E. Paul Torrence, ranges from 0 to an average of 3–4, an excellent of 8, a very unusual score of 12, and an exceptional score of 16.

Conclusion

Our brain fitness questionnaire may have revealed areas of your life that you want to change or improve. They might include the following: becoming more decisive; adopting a healthier diet; starting aerobic exercise; or improving your memory and creativity skills—all of these within the context of designing successful aging strategies for yourself.

If you do want to change any aspect of your life as a result of having completed this quiz, now is the time to review our comments on transforming a Big Bad Habit into a Good New Habit (see chapter 4). Remember the power of metapositive thinking—the power to change yourself for the better.

Torrence Tests

Torrence's tests of creative thinking (see above) were developed to assess the ability of the subject to think divergently and originally. The success of the test-taker will express itself through the divergent thinking facts of: (1) fluency; (2) flexibility; (3) originality; (4) elaboration.

1. **Fluency** expresses itself in the speed and ease with which the test taker can produce creative ideas, whether they come naturally or not, and in a flowing style.

2. **Flexibility** represents the test taker's ability to produce different kinds of ideas and the ability to shift from one approach to another, using a rich variety of strategies.

3. **Originality** represents the ability to produce ideas that are unusual, unique, and far removed from what is normal or commonplace. A person scoring highly in originality may be perceived as nonconforming, but this does not mean that such a person is either erratic or impulsive.

On the contrary, originality is frequently the result of considerable controlled intellectual energy, and it generally shows a capacity for high levels of concentration. The original thinker is more likely to be a renegade from the norm.

4. **Elaboration**. According to Torrence, high scores on elaboration indicate that the subject is able to develop, embroider, embellish, carry out, or otherwise elaborate on ideas. Such persons are likely to demonstrate keenness or sensitivity in observation.

The highest registered scores in the world to date are those of Tony Buzan, who achieved an originality score of 100 percent, and over all four assessed categories in general scored three times higher than the normal register. In preparation for his Torrence test, Tony trained himself physically and honed his Mind Mapping and memory skills before breaking the world record.

Creativity, like any other mental skill, can be taught and learned.

World Memory Challenges

Here is a selection of challenges tried by the World Memory Champions. The time available in the championship is given in parentheses. If you want to try any of them yourself, get a friend to help you with these, acting as an examiner.

RANDOM WORDS (15 MINUTES)

Random words are presented in numbered columns of 50. Contestants need to recall words by writing them down in sequence. The columns are scored as follows: no mistakes scores 50 points, one mistake scores 25 points, and more than one mistake scores zero points. The column scores are totaled for an overall result.

SPOKEN NUMBERS (30 MINUTES)

Contestants listen to 100 numbers between 1 and 100 recited randomly. They must write them down in the order they were recited. A contestant's score is the number of numbers recalled correctly before making a mistake. So if you recall the first 30 numbers in the correct order, and you get the 31st number wrong, your score is 30. The procedure is repeated three times. Only the best score counts.

CARD RECALL (ONE HOUR)

Contestants are given one hour to memorize as many of 12 packs of cards as they can. No mistakes in a pack of cards scores 52 points.

One mistake scores 26 points, and more than one mistake scores zero points.

SPEED CARD RECALL (5 MINUTES)

Contestants are handed a pack of cards shuffled by the arbiter. Stopwatches are set to zero and started at the same time. When contestants have finished memorizing the pack, they raise their hand, and the watch is stopped. Contestants score only the number of cards they recall correctly—for example, remembering the whole pack in one minute, but failing on the 25th card, scores 24 points.

POEM (15 MINUTES)

Contestants are given 40 lines of text to memorize a poem specially written for the event. They then recall this text by writing it down, including the punctuation. If a contestant makes any error in a line, that line is scored as zero. A perfect line scores as one point.

This poem, deliberately constructed to be difficult to remember, was used for the poetry competition at the World Memory Championship in London in 1995. It was written for the occasion by the late Ted Hughes, poet laureate of the U.K.

The Blackened Pearl

A charred and cheeky jackdaw, no respecter
Of rank or person, is pecking the heart
off your epaulette. And grinding his teeth
A sleeper tries to wake. A city of torches
Casts the black and blacker shadow
Of a beast with two backs
Into his fiery eyes. See, the dark sea
Is moving like a fleet, sinister
Under its flag of sky with a star
And a crescent moon. An African witch
Has danced a pentacle
In the dew. And a father blindfolded,
Wobbles like a top inside it, reaching
Into empty air to catch
His dodgy daughter. He offers her a purse
Crammed with Venetian ducats
And the family pearls. A black hand
Snatches it off him. A man with a cloven hoof,

Masked as a devil, hurries away
Carrying a donkey. See, the sea-thunder
Tosses ashore a chest that spills treasures,
Cod's heads and salmon's tails. But the spider
Hauling its net, finds what it hoped for—a fly!
He contorts his mask, he is not seasick.
Belly-full of poisons he conducts
The drinking and singing till two drunkards
Roll a huge bell down hill.
A devil in black jumps out of it, furious,
Flogs everybody with the rags of a bagpipe
Then calls for perfect silence—which appears
As a bride in a nightgown.
A hawk on her shoulder
Slips away, behind a hedge, and leaves her
Feeding a roasted fowl to a green-eyed monster.
A toad, chewed and spewed out,
Crawls on to her handkerchief and squats,
Masticating strawberries. A tooth
Runs through the house in its sleep
Screaming with pain and babbling secrets.
Two men kneel to pray in a flash of lightning—
They are like two mummies hands wiping the sweat
Off each other with a napkin. Like a raven
Sitting on a cataleptic. Like a dog
Champing and swallowing a nose. Like an eye
Weeping a tear of burning sulphur. Now the whole world,
A pearl pendant between breasts,
Goes under honeysuckle, all are drugged with the scent.
Even the honeysuckle feels drowsy

As a gloved hand pulls out a sword
In the shade of a willow, and a man falls,
Hit by a dove. A red rose, full open
Deepens to black, then pales.
A bed, steered by two dead women,
Tilts over the brink of a cataract
Of liquid flame. The black hand salutes us
Flings a pearl into the pool of fire
Then plunges after it, where a salamander,
Green-eyed and the size of a crocodile,
Swirls in the unplumbed blaze, grabbing the bodies—
Their innocence and their guilt equally spicy.

Memory Champions such as Dominic O'Brien and Jonathan Hancock regularly score 100 percent within the allotted time in such tests—the main exception being the poetry, which tends to be the most difficult to recall.

What Should I Do Now?

1. Learn a mind sport, such as chess, go, or bridge. You can either play against friends or competitively, or you can treat the games as logic problems (solving positions in newspapers and magazines) in order to exercise your grey cells.

2. Hone your memory skills, using the classical techniques of memory theaters described in chapter 11.

3. Develop original perspectives on problems or questions that are facing you. Use the associative power of Mind Maps to give you new slants and angles and unleash the

untapped reservoirs of your own creative force. Fresh ideas will then flow freely.

4. Try our memory tests, asking a friend or relation to help, especially on the random words and spoken numbers tests.

5. If you are remembering one pack of cards for the first time, here is a hint: use the classical memory technique— for instance, a theater or a journey—and assign each card a personality and a part to play. Then flip through the deck and weave the cards into your narrative.

Brain Flash
Game Skills Important to Business

Skill at backgammon, bridge, or chess may well get you further along the career path than your college degree or social connections. . . . excellence in playing games of skill is a reasonably accurate predictor of success—perhaps more accurate than a Harvard MBA.

Whether the game is bridge, backgammon, or chess, at the top levels of play, the skills developed are all vitally important in business. Among them are: discipline, memory, coolness under pressure, psychological insightfulness, a readiness to stick to strategy even when it produces losing streaks in the short run, and rapid intuitive calculation of probabilities—of spotting opportunities and balancing risks against rewards.

—*Forbes* magazine

CHAPTER 14

Stepping Up to the Challenge:

What the Future Has in Store

You cannot fight against the future. Time is on our side.
—WILLIAM GLADSTONE

So far we have concentrated on you as an individual. In this final chapter, we make our predictions for the future based on our analysis of the direction in which society as a whole is progressing.

We look at varying visions of the future: prematurely enforced retirement and the failure of the state to provide for the elderly balanced against ongoing self-reliance and triumphs of technology over seemingly natural human limitations. We even examine the mixed blessing of the possibility of virtual immortality through nanotechnology and genetic engineering. We show that the frontiers are not closing in, but are opening up. All you have to do is take advantage of the opportunities that arise and continually stimulate yourself to achieve your full potential.

**Brain Flash
A Vision of the Future**

Spectacular advances in medicine and technology. The elimination of most life-threatening cancers through the mapping of human DNA. . . . Women being able to give birth well into their seventies.

—*Tomorrow's World*, BBC TV Series

Open Frontiers:
The Exponentially Changing Future

We are living in a world of dramatically accelerating change. It took billions of years for primeval bacteria in the ooze of the first oceans to evolve into animal life. It then took hundreds of millions of years for dinosaurs to develop, rule the earth, and vanish. It has taken maybe a couple of million years for humans and human culture to establish themselves, but, incredibly, it is only in the last 200 years or so that we have created any form of conveyance faster than the horse or sail power. Over the last half century, scientific developments have come at breakneck speed: first, the discovery of nuclear energy; then space travel, microcomputers, the Internet, and more. And it is only in the most recent times that we have started to understand the workings of our own brains.

Ever more speedy change is promised in the forthcoming patterns of our social existence, in medicine, economics, environment, and technology. We can even aspire now, through the workings of nanotechnology, to alter systems at the molecular level, rearrange matter, and rewrite genetic codes.

In this chapter, we examine some visions of the future and look at the risks and challenges that it may hold for an aging population.

First, here are some views expressed by Professor Marvin Minsky of the Massachusetts Institute of Technology (MIT). Professor Minsky is widely acknowledged as one of the patriarchs of artificial intelligence (AI). We spoke to him in Boston when he opened the second Man versus Machine World Draughts Championship, which the coauthors organized, between Marion Tinsley and the Chinook computer program.

Everyone wants wisdom and wealth, but our bodies may give out before we achieve them. To lengthen our lives and improve our minds, we'll need to transform our bodies and brains. To that end, we first must see how normal Darwinian evolution brought us to where we are. Then we can look to future techniques to obtain replacements for worn body parts, to solve most problems of failing health. Next, we'll seek wisdom by augmenting our brains and, eventually, by replacing them—with the use of nanotechnology. Then, once delivered from the limitations of biology, we'll have to decide on the lengths of our lives—with the option of immortality—as well as to choose among other, unimagined capabilities. In such a future, attaining wealth will not be a problem: the trouble will be controlling it. Obviously, such changes are hard to envision, and many thinkers still argue that such advances are impossible—particularly in the domain of artificial intelligence. But the sciences needed to enact this transition are already in the making, and it's time to consider what this new role will be like.

In recent times we've learned a lot about health and how to maintain it. We have thousands of specific ways to treat particular diseases and disabilities. However, we do not seem to have increased the length of our maximum lifespan.

Benjamin Franklin lived for 84 years, and, except in popular legends, no one has ever lived twice that long. According to the estimates of Roy Walford, Professor of Pathology at UCLA Medical School, the average human lifespan was about 22 years in ancient Rome, about 50 in the developed countries in 1900 and today stands at about 75. Still, the peaks on each curve seem to terminate sharply near 115 years. Centuries of improvements in health care have had no effect on a recorded maximum of 120.

A few centenarians have broken through that 120 barrier, but our life spans do seem to be limited. Why? Professor Minsky continued:

The answer is simple. Natural selection favors the genes of those with the most descendants. Those numbers tend to grow exponentially with the number of generations—and so this favors the genes of those who reproduce at earlier ages. Furthermore, evolution does not usually favor genes that lengthen lives beyond the amount adults need to care for their young. Indeed, it may even favor offspring who do not have to compete with living parents. Such competition could even promote the accumulation of genes that cause death.

For example, after spawning, the Mediterranean octopus promptly stops eating and starves to death. If we remove a certain gland, though, the octopus continues to eat, and lives twice as long. Many other animals are programmed to die soon after they cease reproducing. Exceptions to this include those long-lived animals, like ourselves and the elephants, whose progeny learn so much from the social transmission of accumulated knowledge.

We humans appear to be the longest-lived warm-blooded animals. What selective pressure might have led to our present longevity? This is related to wisdom! Among all mammals, our infants are the most poorly equipped to survive by themselves. Hence, we need our parents to care for us and to pass on survival tips. Why do we tend to live twice as long as our other primate relatives? Perhaps because our helplessness became so extreme that we needed the wisdom of grandparents, too.

Whatever the unknown future may bring, already we're changing the rules that made us. Although most of us will be fearful of change, others will surely want to escape from our present limitations. I tried out these ideas on several groups and had them respond to informal polls. I was amazed to find that at least three-quarters of the audience were opposed to the prospect of much longer lives. Many people seemed to feel that our lifespans were already too long. "Why would anyone want to live for five hundred years?" "Wouldn't it be boring?" "What if you outlived all your friends?" "What would you do with all that time?"

My scientist friends showed few such concerns. "There are countless things that I want to find out, and so many problems I want to solve, that I could use many centuries." Certainly, immortality would seem unattractive if it meant endless infirmity, debility, and dependency upon others—but we're assuming a state of perfect health.

Fascinating insights from a top scientist at the cutting edge of current thinking about aging. Now we examine other visions of the future.

Brain Flash
Another Vision of the Future

The vision of an increasingly dependent elderly population making unsustainable demands on public spending haunts the Western world. In Britain as well as Germany, Japan, America, France, and Italy, the assumption is that, sometime beyond the turn of the century, there will be too few people in work to support the ever bigger, older, and frailer group of pensioners. Either taxes will have to rise, or pensions will have to fall, if government debt is to remain manageable.

—The Times

The answer, surely, on the individual level is to set up your own business and never retire.

Peering into the Future

Now, perhaps more than in the past several decades, you will need to stay fit both mentally and physically to be able to secure a quality life for yourself in your later years. In this section, we make a few predictions about changes in several key areas of business, society, and government that are likely to affect your life. This early warning is not intended to inspire fear about the future but to motivate you to prepare for these changes while you can still improve your future outcomes.

Portable retirement plans. When you want to know what is in store for the future, look to California. California's CalSavers program is a mandatory retirement savings program that requires all employers with five or more employees to provide a retirement plan for their workers or register for the CalSavers plan and facilitate the employees' contributions to individual retirement accounts (IRAs). CalSavers plans follow the employee to ensure a greater retirement security as employees change jobs. Although we advise never to retire, having a sufficient retirement nest egg of your own will give you the freedom to pursue the opportunities you desire later in life instead of settling for whatever job openings are available.

A growing gig economy. *You'll switch jobs often—so develop your own versatility.* As the current jargon has it, you'll have a portfolio of skills. In your bag will surely be improved computer literacy, along with some programming skills. You'll still specialize, but in a spread of subjects. Marketing executives will be vulnerable if, say, they restrict their knowledge to the motor industry; they would be better off adding skills in computers and coding too. The suggestion is that you'll be employed on demand for perhaps a year or two, then out of work for a while—sometimes at your choosing, in the form of a career break.

Government-funded retirement and healthcare. *Don't count on it.* Increasingly, governments around the world are having to borrow money to fund their entitlement programs as their populations grow older and fewer younger working people are available to pay for these programs. We are seeing more and more reports in the news about the inevitability of such programs going bankrupt. Even if they remain solvent, governments will need to reduce the benefits, either by scaling them back or increasing the retirement age. The message: don't rely on the government to take care of you in your old age.

Houses—will you rent or buy? You'll still want to buy your own home, but you may well rent for longer before you have children. When you do buy, you'll be wary of mortgaging yourselves to the hilt. You'll look for green space, which will increasingly command a premium. And communication technology will be almost as critical as trains and buses.

Energy costs on the rise. Cheap, clean energy is the goal, but don't hold your breath. The costs of oil and natural gas will continue to rise as supplies dwindle and governments discourage the burning of fossil fuels. At the same time, transition to technology for producing cleaner energy and building the infrastructure to distribute it will continue to drive up energy costs, which increases the cost of *everything.* If you're thinking of retiring on a fixed income, these rising costs can seriously undermine your plans.

Brain Flash
Working-Life Expectancies Have Been
Turned Upside-Down by Early Achievers

Life begins at forty, and so, for an increasing number of high-flyers, does eminence. We are now witnessing the incredible shrinking career—with many people in their early forties doing jobs that used to be reserved for those in their fifties or sixties. Not only rock stars, tennis players, and policemen seem young these days; so do Prime Ministers, Leaders of the Opposition and chief executives of high street banks.

What will these still-youthful chief executives do when they have run out of drive and initiative? Orchestrating a permanent revolution must pall after a decade or so at the top, but they will be way off retirement age. They will not have had the wedge-shaped careers that their fathers experienced: gradual promotion from their twenties to their sixties, followed by sudden retirement. The new shape of careers is triangular, with an apex in the middle.

How people cope with the downward slope will vary enormously. Some will be delighted to have the opportunity to pursue interests that they never could before. Some might make a decent living from consultancy, part-time chairmanship, and directorships: the "portfolio" approach to work.

Others, however, may become bitter: "The problem is that most people can't get off the moving staircase until they fall off it. Sometimes they're concerned about the loneliness of retirement and they don't have enough to do. That prospect is very frightening."

—The Times of London

The good news: you'll live longer. Men can now expect to live on average to seventy-four, and women to eighty, although obviously many of us will live far longer. In the future, that average will extend itself to an as yet unknown age. And in general, you'll lose weight, eat healthier foods (less sugar and dairy produce, more salads and fresh fruit), and exercise more.

The overall trend is clearly toward greater personal self-reliance.

Conclusion

We have reached the conclusion of this book, and it is time to summarize our message. Over the course of the preceding chapters, we have shown you how your brain circuitry can physically improve as you age, how your memory need not fail with increasing years—indeed, it can (and should) improve. We have demonstrated important mental fitness techniques, such as TEFCAS, metapositive thinking, Mind Mapping, and mnemonics, and we have stressed the paramount importance of self-challenge. We have also introduced you to renegades from the norm, who are constantly challenging themselves in later years. *You can do this too.* This is your future!

Design Your Own Aging Strategy

Remember the single most vital lesson in this book: *your brain cells are not inevitably dying off every day.* The important point is the interconnectivity between your brain cells and your power to make associations and learn new things. You can continue to multiply this capacity.

The more your brain is stimulated and challenged, the greater its potential to achieve at any age. The latest medical research indicates that such stimulation is the best defense you can adopt against Alzheimer's disease, dementia, and strokes.

Practical Steps

Look after your physical and mental health. Remember: your brain is connected to your body. If you smoke, try to cut down and then give up entirely. If you drink heavily, cut down. Have a thorough annual physical exam. Ask your doctor what your ideal weight is and then work to achieve it. Start physical exercise and achieve greater mental clarity by taking up mind sports such as chess, Scrabble, checkers, bridge, or go.

Be aware of the phenomenal power of your own brain. It is the most complex structure that we know of in the universe. Use Mind Maps to harness and deploy your full set of cortical resources and skills—to organize your thoughts, help you to communicate, and improve your memory and recall of important facts and ideas.

Remember: the more you learn, the easier it is to learn more. Follow our simple tips in chapter 3 on speed-reading and improving your memory through mnemonics.

Change Your Habits

Mobilize metapositive thinking and TEFCAS to change yourself for the better, to ditch harmful old habits and acquire good new ones. Use the process: Trial, Event, Feedback, Check, Adjust, Success.

Remember the main message of metapositive thinking: it is never too late to start. This is true whether you are taking up a challenging new mental exercise, developing a new skill, developing a superpower memory, trying a new form of exercise, sport, or martial art, or cutting back on alcohol, cigarettes, or overeating.

In summary, as you age, commit yourself to becoming a renegade from the norm.

The Tovey Solution

Next, we have distilled six golden rules from the notable experiences related by the late Sir Brian Tovey, a renowned British intelligence analyst, for you to follow as you begin your quest to achieve more as you get older. Here they are:

1. Keep yourself physically and mentally at a fitness peak.
2. Prepare for change and welcome it.
3. Challenge yourself. Be ready to take the leap and reinvent yourself.
4. Have the courage to be your own master—whatever your age.
5. Work with a loving and supportive ally (if possible).
6. Love what you do and do what you love. Never retire!

Truth versus Misconception

On a piece of blank paper, draw your own image of "age."

In surveys conducted during the last twenty years, when tens of thousands of individuals were asked to draw their images of age, 80–100 percent drew negative images. These same individuals were then asked if they knew anyone of seventy-five or older who did *not* fit this negative category.

Encouragingly (and not surprisingly!), virtually everyone in the audience raised his or her hand, indicating that there are millions of individuals who are the statistical anomalies mentioned in chapter 4: the renegades from the norm.

As you now know, the brain is drawn toward the image it perceives. If you view age in a morbid and depressing way, you will subconsciously guide your own life in that direction, like a missile heading directly toward its own doom.

If you found yourself drawing a walking stick, a skull and crossbones, or a gravestone, circle it, put an exclamation mark by the side, and commit that image to your memory as the last time you ever thought of age in this way. Your ideal image would have been a smiling face, a world traveler, a healthy and sensuous individual, an athlete, a mountain climber, or a multimillionaire!

All the questions raised in the introduction to this book have now been answered, and in each case we have recommended accessible, positive, concrete, and practical steps—none of them too obscure or difficult to understand and achieve. Every one of you who has read the book should have found an inspirational message, one that encourages you to improve with age and shows, simply and clearly, how you can do it yourself.

The Century of the Brain

The years 1990–1999 were designated the "Decade of the Brain" by former US president George W. Bush "to enhance public awareness of the benefits to be derived from brain research." We applaud any efforts to increase awareness about brain health and encourage people to care for their brains, but a single decade is only a start. We would like to declare the twenty-first century the "Century of the Brain."

Technology is making great leaps in brain research, providing more and more insight into both brain structure and function. Just the other day, we read a study published in the January 2022 edition of the *Proceedings of the National Academy of Sciences* about a research team at the University of Southern California that was able to visualize memories forming in the brains of laboratory fish. We can now see in real time how neuronal networks form in response to perceptions and experiences.

We encourage you to follow the latest research on brain health, function, and development. It not only keeps you well-informed while stimulating your own brain cells but also provides the encouragement and motivation necessary to continue building and strengthening your own neural networks.

Further Reading

By Raymond Keene, OBE

Among the 85 books that grand master Raymond Keene has written on chess and mind sports in general, the following are particularly recommended:

Understanding the Caro-Kann Defense. Compiled by three grand masters and two international masters, this scholarly treatise explains in depth the thinking behind a defense that has been a favorite of champions such as Capablanca, Botvinnik, Petrosian, and Karpov.

Flank Openings: A Study of Reti's Opening, the Catalan, English and King's Indian Attack Complex: Fourth Edition. Traditional chess openings emphasize control of the center. Flank openings are opening systems first developed by such players as Reti and Nimzowitsch, in which the player of the white pieces concedes control of the center to Black, but then seeks to undermine the center and cause it to collapse with attacks from the sides. Raymond Keene explains the concepts and ideas behind these chess opening systems.

Batsford Chess Openings II. This is the standard one-volume reference work on chess openings. Since the first edition was published in 1982, the book has sold more than

100,000 copies. The coauthor is the World Chess Champion, Garry Kasparov.

Chess for Absolute Beginners. The ideal introduction to chess, perfect for children and adults alike, with simple, clear, and easy-to-understand diagrams in color by artist Barry Martin.

By Raymond Keen and Tony Buzan

Buzan's Book of Genius, and How to Unleash Your Own. All the advice you need to fulfill your potential and make the most of your mental skills.

By Tony Buzan

Mind Map Mastery: The Complete Guide to Learning and using the Most Powerful Thinking Tool in the Universe The comprehensive guide to Mind Mapping by its originator. Exciting new ways to use and improve your memory, concentration, and creativity in planning and structuring thought on all levels.

Use Your Head. The classic BBC best seller, which has sold over a million copies. Foundation learning skills and Mind Mapping explained by their inventor. Latest information on your brain's functioning, enabling you to learn how to learn more effectively.

Use Your Memory. An encyclopedia of brain-related memory techniques. Provides easy-to-manage techniques for remembering names, faces, places, jokes, telephone numbers, and everything else you want or need to remember.

Speed/Range Reading. Establish a range of reading speeds up to 10,000 words per minute with good comprehension. Self-checks and practical exercises throughout.

Make the Most of Your Mind (paperback); *Harnessing the Parabrain* (hardcover). A complete course dealing with reading, memory number skills, logic, vision, listening, and study. Builds to the complete Mind Map Organic Study Technique.

To make the most of your mind at any age, contact the one-stop shop for all brain-related courses and products: TonyBuzan.com.

About the Author

Tony Buzan (June 2, 1942–April 13, 2019) was an English author and education consultant who popularized the idea of mental literacy, radiant thinking, and a technique called Mind Mapping. His was the mind behind Mind Maps® and the concepts of Mental Literacy and Metapositive Thinking. He also founded the International Brain Clubs and was responsible for many developments in the theory and advancement of mnemonic systems and creativity.

Buzan was editor of the *International Journal of MENSA* (the high IQ Society) and also was the holder of the world's highest creativity IQ. Among the members of the Young President's Organization, he was affectionately known as "Mr. Brain."

He was a prolific writer, authoring more than 14 books (most on the brain, creativity, learning, and memory, along with one volume of poetry). His books, which include *Use Both Sides of Your Brain, Use Your Perfect, Memory, Make the Most of Your Mind, and Speed-Reading,* have been published in 50 countries and translated into 20 languages. *Use Both Sides of Your Brain* surpassed worldwide sales of 1 million and is a standard introductory text for staff training within IBM, General Motors, EDS, Fluor Daniel, and Digital Equipment Corporation, and for students of the Open University.

Tony Buzan was an international media star who featured in, presented, and coproduced many satellite broadcasts, television, video, and radio programs, both national and international, including the record-breaking *Use Your Head* series (BBC TV) and the *Open Mind* series (ITV); *The Enchanted Loom*, a one-hour feature documentary on the brain; numerous talk shows; and a video series called *Improving Mental Performance*—a three-part training package that introduced the major elements of his work to the international business community.

He was an advisor to governments and multinational organizations, including BP, Barclays International, Bell Telephone, AT&T, Rank Xerox, and Nabisco, and was a regular lecturer at leading international universities and schools.

Buzan was also an advisor to international Olympic coaches and athletes and to the British Olympic Rowing Squad as well as the British Olympic Chess Squads. He was a Fellow of the Institute of Training and Development, the Jamaican Institute of Management, and the Swedish Management Group, and was an elected member of the International Council of Psychologists. He was a member of the Institute of Directors, a Freeman of the City of London, and a Patron of the Young Entrepreneurs' Societies of both Bristol and Cambridge universities. Adding to his list of honors, including the YPO Leadership Award, was his recognition by Electronic Data Systems with the Eagle Catcher Award—given to those who attempt the impossible and achieve it!

Printed in the USA
CPSIA information can be obtained
at www.ICGtesting.com
JSHW010335090923
48117JS00010B/16

9 781722 506384